HOW TO BE A BEAUTIFUL WOMAN

AND OTHER VITAL WISDOM FOR YOU WHATEVER YOUR SEX

Esther Stasek

SEVEN STARS PUBLISHING
CLEVELAND, OHIO
1993

HOW TO BE A BEAUTIFUL WOMAN

AND OTHER VITAL WISDOM FOR YOU
WHATEVER YOUR SEX

Esther Stasek

Library of Congress Catalog Card Number: 92-83953
Stasek, Esther
  HOW TO BE A BEAUTIFUL WOMAN
  And Other Vital Wisdom For
  You Whatever Your Sex
1. Humor
2. Satire
Printed in the United States of America
ISBN 0-9635825-0-X

To my Husband, Alfred

My Club Sisters, THE GEMS

And the Good Ol' Bunch at the Bank

TABLE OF CONTENTS

TABLE OF CONTENTS, Cont'd.

EXPLANATION

Other books have an *Introduction*, a *Foreword* and maybe even a *Preface*. This one does not need such redundancies. This one needs an **Explanation**.

Every essay in here is meant to entertain you. To give you smiles, chuckles and laughs, and even some novel ideas. But some of these writings are satirical, while others are basically sincere.

Thus, so that confusion doesn't set in when you go from one to another, try to consider them as being like chocolates in one of those assortment boxes:

They come in a variety of kinds and flavors--some smooth, some nutty.

It's barely possible you might take a bite of one and then (God forbid) feel like spitting it out into the sink, like my kids used to do with the coconut kind.

But you'll probably find that many of these are delicious, just to your taste.

So look them over and take your pick. Guaranteed non-fattening.

EXERCISE is Not a Dirty Word

Quicky questions:

If you get the chance, do you take more naps than the Little Ones in your family do?

Do you avoid getting down on the floor because it's such a huffy struggle to get up again?

Do you sleep on one side all night because it's a burden to turn yourself over?

Are you compelled to go find someone to help when you have a container of jelly or motor oil to unscrew?

Do you send a family member to answer the phone or bring in the mail because when you've just got comfortable in a chair, you're not about to leave your seat to do anything else for the rest of the day?

Do you find your clothes growing smaller, the number on the scales growing larger, but the amount you eat staying just about the same? Does this stir up your wishful thinking that maybe someone's altering your clothes or playing games with the scales?

If you're in normal health but answer yes to these nosy queries, you have a problem. But, lucky for you, I'm here to offer you the solution--EXERCISE! (Like as if you never heard of it before.)

BUT, you probably protest, there are too many things to prevent people from exercising. What about these miserable events we're always hearing about?:

- joggers dropping dead with heart attacks,
- cyclists getting chased by dogs and flipped by cars,
- athletes who stop their active exercising for a few days having their muscles turn to fat before their very eyes,

- calisthenics wreaking havoc on people's joints,
- weightlifting giving women big ugly muscles and men a hernia,
- and you KNOW what can happen to people swimming in deep water.

So although you probably COULD grudgingly find time to indulge in more or less regular exercise if you really had to, what are you supposed to do that's SAFE?

Surely you've heard of people who are on the phone so much, one day their phone grows onto their ear and becomes permanently attached? This also happens to backsides, which become permanently stuck to seat cushions.

It can happen even if you work outside the home and only weld yourself to the cushion during evenings and weekends! It's a dreadful medical disorder sweeping the country, mostly unheard of before the Twentieth Century, banally labeled "Lack-of-real-exercise".

If you hope to avoid this sneaky disease, check out the assorted kinds of exercises listed below. Knowing how lethargic you may feel, I've done all the hard work for you; all you have to do is read. Surely there's SOMETHING in here you might be able to do without harming or killing yourself.

Calisthenics

The modern way is called "low impact". This means you don't stomp your feet hard or leap very high, so your joints should be unharmed. On TV this looks like a lot of fun because you see everyone grinning through the sweat. While your leader barks out unintelligible instructions, you twist, bend, stretch, bounce, and make lewd gestures to music.

Although most of the motions performed make you wonder how they accomplish anything at all, calisthenics supposedly will cause you to become flexible and supple, able to reach high shelves, twirl swiftly around to catch a child or an employee doing wrong, zip your own back zippers, even scrub your own back.

Large numbers of people enter into these activities, none of which are called CALISTHENICS anymore but have clever names like Frolic-Ercize or Flex & Sweat. They're offered in schools, Y's, and spas all over town.

When their classes end, the pupils go home and ignore all further exertion, cheerful in the belief that they did something for their bodies. For instance, their flab (which is still there) seems to have become a tad firmer, and their waistline seems almost to have shrunk.

Weight Training

This too looks like fun, proficiently hefting those weights while learning the whimsical nicknames of the various muscles; nimbly connecting yourself to weighted pulleys so you can work on muscles you never knew you had. If you train several hours a day and lift ridiculously heavy weights, you women MAY develop "manly" muscles, and you men MIGHT get a hernia.

But you know you're not going to drudge like that. You'll be doing well to get your act together for some weight work three times a week, right? Luckily, that's all you need if you want to grow strong enough to lift and change car tires, push snow blowers without falling down under them, haul filled garbage cans, and help move a piano if this opportunity should ever come your way.

Isometrics

This one doesn't seem very fun filled. You push and pull against floors, walls, doorways, or your own limbs. It's a mostly outmoded method for building a few bumps of muscle while you grunt, grimace, turn red, distend your veins and make your neck bulge. However, it could be suitable if your doctor thinks you don't have enough stress in your life and wants you to boost your blood pressure.

Aerobics

This one has so many extraordinary benefits attributed to it, it's hard to believe. Health guidebooks now collectively assert that aerobics will do these remarkable things for you (all without drugs!):

- strengthen your heart,
- hop up your breathing capacity,
- speed up your metabolism so you burn calories faster,
- lower cholesterol in your blood,
- use up adrenalin caused by fright or anger, thus making you feel calm and serene,
- change your consistency from bumpy, lumpy fat to smooth-lined muscle.

So let's hear it for AEROBICS!

But even though it's the wise sluggish person's exertion of choice, there are possible imperfections in the various forms of aerobics, namely:

Jogging

This is the most celebrated aerobic activity. But if done out-doors, it has the most drawbacks. You have to contend with traffic, smog, rain, snow, ice, heat prostration, sunburn, muggers, dogs and bees. It can hurt your feet, knees, and other joints if you overdo it. Jogging on a padded indoor track would be easier on you if you didn't mind paying a robust fee to a spa for the privilege.

Running in Place

This is next in line after jogging, but you may pay for it with sore feet, aching knees, and bounced-about breasts or other parts. Also, the scenery doesn't change, so you could rapidly lose interest in running in place.

Jumping Rope

If done outdoors, you must contend with the weather foiling you, and your neighbors scrutinizing you. Indoors, you'll jar the floor; and if you try it in the basement, the rope will ricochet off the ceiling and smack you on the head.

Cycling

Bicycling has the same outdoor deterrents as jogging, plus you'll have to take a longer route to get the same benefits. Once you get far away from home, you'll be tempted to go shopping or stop in for ice cream, and your family will complain that exercising keeps you away from home too much.

Fastwalking

An inventive new exercise method has sprung up: fastwalking in the malls before the stores open. I discovered this when I went to the mall early one morning and was nearly trampled by several folks in sweatsuits rushing by. It's a neat way to get your aerobics if you live near a mall that allows this sort of commotion, and if you take care not to knock down the customers.

Swimming

This obviously is easy on your joints and feet, and is a suitable (or you might say "swimsuitable") option. But if you don't have your own pool, with some trustworthy person on guard nearby in case you get a cramp or fall asleep, it means traveling 3 or 4 times a week to find an open pool, learning how to swim, letting strangers see your figure faults, and coming home with a damp swimsuit, chlorine-greened hair and pruney fingers.

Housework and Yardwork

Nah. I don't care what you say, this won't give you a regular aerobic workout. (I KNOW many people "chase after" kids. This mainly consists of exercising the throat muscles with yelling, screaming and orating.) Take it from an ex-housewife, mother of seven ex-children: your household, yard and garage chores just won't do it.

You say mopping floors is good? Sure, so you can walk through the kitchen without sticking to the floor.

Vacuuming? It's good too, if you don't want lint, hair and dead-skin scales to take over your dwelling. But it's way too easy.

Washing walls? How often do you do that?

Cooking, ironing, sewing, changing bedding, doing laundry, typing, computing, driving, changing auto fluids, painting the house, trimming hedges, picking zucchini, talking on the phone? Get serious.

Of course, if you want to mow the lawn with a push mower and you have an immense yard and mow it three or four times a week, that might add up to aerobic sessions. And the same idea for snow shoveling--you need a vast set of sidewalks and driveways and a few-days-a-week schedule. But somehow these don't seem to fill the bill as rational ongoing exercises, do they.

The Solution

I've found the perfect solution to your yearning for aerobic exercise, and I'll describe it in seven simple exclamations:
1. After an initial payout of money, it's free forever after!
2. It's indoors, safe and private!
3. It's the famous "low impact". You don't hurt your joints!
4. It takes up time, of course, but you can do other things at the same time!
5. You can be entertained while you're doing it!
6. You can do it mindlessly, without having to count anything!
7. You can wear anything you please!
    I bet you can hardly wait to find out what it is!

No big secret--it's the good old stationary exercise bike. (Did I hear you say *"Oh, Brother!"*?) Hey, it's the perfect aerobic exercise; give it a chance and you'll love it. Unlike all the other aerobic exertions, it's so easy and handy, you'll never be able to find a reason NOT to do it. (Hopefully, that thought inspires you.)

While pedaling away and getting all those wonderful health benefits, you can listen to music, read, watch television, compose a speech. Stationary-bike riders have been known to attach a basket to the bike and use it to hold the afghan they're crocheting while they exercise.

If the stationary biking idea strikes you as being splendid, here's the plan:

1. Have you heard the one about seeing your doctor for his/her endorsement to get into exercise? Go for it. Your doctor may be so impressed he'll applaud you.

2. Look through the aerobics section in the public library and scan some up-to-date books on how to use a bike for conditioning. (Like how long, how hard, and how often.) Then go to a book store and buy the book you liked the best. That's a lot better than trying to memorize it at the library.

3. Visit stores and try out exercise bikes. Don't be embarrassed-- climb up on that seat and pedal those pedals, and be sure to check how to change the pedaling from easy to hard. When you find a bike that's fun to use and you can afford, get it.

4. Before you take the bike home, fight it out with everyone else in the household as to where you're going to keep it. If you want it right in front of the TV set, that might mean removing a sofa and your spouse to the basement. So if YOU end up in the basement, take an old TV set down there, and think of it as your own little private haven where you don't have to apologize to anyone about the pedaling noise or your choice of TV programs.

Some bikes have a device for jerking your arms around while your legs are going. Decide whether you'd rather leave your arms free to fiddle with your radio or book or other hobby. Luckily, a pedal-only bike is all you need for an unblemished aerobic workout.

You'll find that getting and using an exercise bike is one of the best things you ever did for yourself, giving you something to brag about to all your indolent friends.

Soon you'll be able to leap up off the floor and flip over in bed; eagerly get the mail from the mailbox and personally answer the phone; dash, dance, and work without needing naps. Soon you'll lose fat and gain muscle--get slimmer, that is!

Last and best, aerobic exercise will make you FEEL GOOD. Besides winning the lottery, what could be more excellent than that?

Fun Trip Advisory

This is not about packing a hamper of food and a jug of fruit-ade, climbing into the family car and traveling hither and yon till your food runs out or someone whines they wanna go home. That doesn't require instructions.

My husband and I did that for years till the kids grew up and left, and I got my own job and my own money. Then I TRAVELED.

Traveling means going to a specific destination for the purpose of having fun, and involves four obligatory steps:

1. planning
2. getting to the place
3. having the fun
4. going home

1. Planning

Travel Agencies

I once thought that going to a travel agency would be like going to an attorney. (I'd never done either.) After they took your name, address and social security number, they'd answer three questions for a set fee, then charge extra for each added question.

But a travel agency will cheerfully furnish you with all kinds of travel particulars, an armful of beautiful brochures and an agent's card for FREE.

I thought too they might treat you like salespeople I've met who quote a low figure, talk you into buying, then bushwhack you with add-ons that make the charge a lot higher than you thought it was going to be.

Nope. Travel agents come right out and tell you what a trip taken through them will cost. "If you buy the package, it'll come to $450 a day." Act cool, as though $450 a day for eating, sleeping and seeing sights would be a real bargain, and not a horrendous shock to your sense of fairness and your yearly income.

Be prepared for a second, though smaller, jolt when they disclose how much money you should take along for sundries not included in the written trip description. If they don't bring this up, ASK. You want unexpected expenses to be EXPECTED.

Travel Agents

Speaking of individual travel agents, a teeny number of them make you want to scream in their face to get their attention. They seem to be utterly bored with you, consider their job a nuisance, and are pseudo-deaf.

That means they're unaware of what you say because they never actually listen. When you speak to them you can see their eyes wandering everywhere but on you. (Are they hoping to find someone more interesting behind you?)

I told one agent what week I had off and what cruise I wanted to take. I'd made my plans ahead of time, so all she had to do was go to a phone, make the arrangements and give me some papers.

Later I read the paperwork and found she'd set me up for a trip I'd already taken and for a week I had to work.

She finally got me to where I wanted to go, but on reaching there I ripped up her business card and dropped the pieces into the ocean.

There are also agents who are so helpful and nice you feel as if they've become a dear friend and you want to take them home with you for a visit. Try to pick an agent like this by getting their name from someone who prizes them.

Then USE your agent to help you with all the questions and worries that loom in your mind during the seemingly endless interval between signing up for the trip and actually going on it. Except for the one-time flat price, the answers and advice are free.

Travel Information

I love looking at brochures. I can sit and daydream over one for hours. But BEWARE of them. Before reading a brochure, put your mind into gear. Here's a sample description you might find:

"Package includes all-star shows, luxury suites, complete health club, sauna, indoor and outdoor pools, tennis courts, boating, miniature golf, softball, horseback riding, hiking trails." Wow!

"All-star shows". Their idea of a star doesn't necessarily gibe with yours, nor their idea of luxury in "luxury suites." Realize that you're not so much reading FACTS as reading OPINIONS.

The Complete Health Club: usually a single room, smaller than it looked in the brochure, with exercise bikes, mirrors, and some weight machines. When you open the door, you'll likely find muscle types working out, but don't allow a feeling of punyness to make you skulk back out. Barge right in--muscular people are as hospitable as anyone else. You can pedal a bike if you can't get the bulky people away from the weights.

Sauna--people use that word when describing weather that's insufferably hot and humid. How much precious vacation time do you want to dissipate hanging out in a place like that?

18

Pools are fun, of course, especially an indoor one you can slosh in without getting sunburned. As to all those listed sport possibilities, you may think "Oh, look at all the things I can do there!" until you realize you're unlikely to do any of them.

If you don't want to travel stupid, go to the library and study up on the place you want to visit. Or to a book store if you want the very most up-to-date info. There are guidebooks for the entire world.

You'll get a lot more out of your trip if you find out ahead of time what you can see and do there. Like Hawaii--do you just GO there and sit on a beach soaking up skin cancer? No! After you've studied your brochures, scan some books.

2. Getting To the Place

The trip there should be fun, so don't drive. Let someone else do the driving or the flying while you sit back, survey the scenery and gnaw on a snack.

Planes

As soon as possible, get signed up for the flight, asking for a seat by a window but not over a wing. You can't see through a wing.

You'll love a plane ride! As you build up speed, the scenery rushes past faster and faster, till the plane suddenly leaves the ground and you're actually flying.

I make a fool of myself during takeoff by giggling and stifling squeals, then grin absurdly for several minutes after we're up in the clouds. (I can't help it, and my traveling companions can just pretend they don't know me.)

Scared or not, let go and enjoy it. On a plane, unless you're flying it yourself, what else CAN you do? Decide ahead of time that, no matter what happens on your trip, you're going to enjoy it because you PAID for it.

It took me only one flight to become addicted to looking out the window. If you're like that, try to travel with others who don't mind you hogging the window. Or if your companion should also insist on the window seat, insist on taking turns.

The higher you go, the slower the scenery below passes, till you think maybe the plane has stopped dead and is about to fall back down. But no; you pass through clouds, rise ABOVE the clouds and then you know you're really on your way.

Bus, Train

You can also stay on the ground and be propelled to your destination by bus or train; or the trip on the bus or train can be the vacation itself. Use whatever travel mode you think might make YOU want to giggle, squeal or beam uncontrollably.

Ships

Plainly, a cruise is different from a land trip. You don't change hotel rooms from city to city, but just keep the one stateroom the whole time. No multiple packing and unpacking. No spending half your time trying to remember which bag or drawer you put something in the last time you used it, or which way is the pool.

Although you sleep in the same bed every night (and it sways SO nicely you think you're in a baby cradle), almost every day you're in a different part of the world. After breakfast you step out onto the gangplank and enter a land you never saw before!

Cruise lines boast about PAMPERING you. Have you ever stopped to cogitate on what that actually means? Or if it's something you'd really want?

First off, it doesn't mean putting a plastic-covered paper diaper on you, but you knew that, didn't you. I looked it up. It means "to baby, coddle, humor, indulge, overindulge, or spoil."

Pampering sounds as though it might be nice if you happen to be the helpless sort, or if it flatters you to be treated the way you imagine rich people are.

When I went on a cruise, I watched for signs of being pampered. One incident I noticed that might be construed as pampering was the waiter opening a big fancily-folded linen napkin and placing it on my lap at the start of each meal. I noted later, when I wiped my mouth, that the napkin really wasn't too heavy for me to have unfolded and put on my lap by myself.

Besides our waiter, a gentleman stood at our table and opened a bottle of wine my travel agent had pre-ordered for me. (She wanted me to remember her fondly.) He was called the Wine Steward. (Why not then a meat steward to cut our meat or a salad steward to dress our salad?) I did appreciate this little service, since I flinch and blink when I have to pull out a cork.

But then he poured some of the wine into my glass, handed it to me and watched me as I took a sip. Everyone else at the table sat back and watched too. I don't LIKE being watched carefully when I do ANYTHING. And being not much of a drinker but more an eater, I wanted to get started on my steak, so I plunked down the glass and looked at the steward with polite impatience. (That's a difficult trick.)

Later I found out this is a pampering ritual. The wine steward wants you to smell, taste, and feel the wine in your mouth and then give him your meritorious opinion: The wine is delightful--please pour some in everyone's glass; or This stuff is vinegar--pour it out a porthole. For this pampering, you are to tip him at the end of the trip, which doesn't seem very pampery to me.

You may think me low-class, but I don't want a steward pouring wine for me and awaiting my reaction as though I'm the Queen of Sheba. I'm just as happy to drink diet pop, skim milk or coffee with a meal. These, obviously, don't have corks.

And I hate linen napkins. They just don't do the job of soaking up grease and holding crumbs the way good old paper napkins do. They also fall open from their own weight and reveal my lipstick smears and whatever food missed the mark. Too, I feel silly when the waiter places the napkin on my lap. Leave my lap alone.

Although I enjoyed cruising immensely, I sensed no other pampering on the trip. We weren't babied, coddled, spoiled, or overindulged. But we WERE entertained, enlightened, amused and overfed. In fact, it seemed that every few minutes someone was saying "Let's go, it's time to eat." (No it wasn't me!)

3. Having The Fun

Let's face it--a large part of a trip anywhere at all entails your everyday chores of eating, bathing and sleeping, so they should be thought about ahead of time.

Eating

For the person who often has to cook for a family, eating out at a restaurant is a real treat. You can choose what you fancy, and someone else has to cook it and clean up after you. I've always considered THAT pampering.

But, on a land trip, eating at a restaurant day after day becomes irksome. The worst part is, it's expensive. Sometimes too, all you really crave is to reach into a cupboard and get some crackers and peanut butter. Not many restaurants will let you do that.

There are two ways to get around eating at full-service restaurants all the time on your trip. First, go to some little corner store (all towns have them), and buy a tiny stash of groceries to keep in your room. This is not the time to "save money" by buying the giant economy size of anything.

Second. I know people who turn purple and foam at the mouth when I mention this, but here it is: As soon as you've settled your belongings into your hotel room, take a walk and find the nearest McDonald's or close facsimile.

WHAT?--eat at a Fast Food joint on your vacation in an exotic part of the world?! Yeah--why not?

• I've compared meals in expensive restaurants and those at the Fast Food, and where the menus coincide it's the same food.

• At the FF, no one's hovering over you asking if all is well so you'll remember to give them a tip.

• The food's not served on a dish others have eaten from--it's in a brand new plastic or cardboard container.

• To live up to their reputation, they get your food to you FAST, while you're still hungry and can remember what you ordered.

• Is it gauche to add that it costs only one-fourth or -fifth of what it does at the hotel or other restaurant?

• And the FF gives paper napkins which, as you already know, work much better than linen ones.

Sleeping and Bathing

If in your travels you sleep in a tent, camper or bunk house, I admire your fortitude. But I advise LUXURY in your sleeping arrangements: a bed with a real mattress in a genuine room where no bears or flying critters can find entry.

I also highly recommend an indoor bathroom containing a toilet that indeed flushes, a sink with drinkable water, and a tub or shower with enough hot water to actually bathe in.

Ranging Around the Place--Planned vs. Haphazard

Some travelers, usually the teen & 20's crowd, enjoy the idea of hopping off the plane in a strange town, jumping into a rental car and taking off into the wild blue yonder with only a map to guide them.

Many towns must run out of money and can't finish proposed projects, because maps always depict a number of roads where no roads exist. They FAIL to show what parts of which towns you should steer clear of if you don't want to get mugged. So don't rely on a map unless you don't care where in heck you're going but just like to use up gasoline.

You also can't fully bank on what the natives tell you, even if they speak your language and you can understand each other's accent. (On one Caribbean Island we heard inhabitants talking unintelligibly, so we asked one what language they speak there. He said very indignantly "ENGLISH!")

People try to be helpful, but they may give you a bum steer. I've innocently but stupidly done that to travelers myself in my own neighborhood, so I'm not blaming anyone.

To avoid haphazard waste of good vacation time, try my personal favorite, the Escorted Tour, the land version of the Cruise. You're met at the airport by a person holding up a sign with your tour company's name in big bold letters, so you can't miss them.

After they collect all the people who'll be traveling in your group, they take you to your luggage, then to a bus that whisks you and your luggage to your hotel.

Every day it goes like that. You don't have to worry about anything. You hardly even have to remember your escort's face and name, because their job is to remember yours. You can ask them all sorts of dumb questions about the area, and (as they always impishly tell you) they'll answer your every query even if they have to make up something.

If it sounds like you won't have any time to yourself, think again. Each day's tour or other activity has a specified end, leaving you with plenty of time to lounge by the pool, wander around at random, or deplete your travelers checks in shops.

What To Do

If you're on an island, take the Circle Island Tour. You'll be driven around in a van or bus to see highlights of the whole place, with a stop for lunch at some novel eatery, then another stop at the best tourist-trap shop around. (It's fun, and it's unlikely anyone will force you to buy anything.)

Your driver, anticipating a tip at the end, will stop whenever someone needs to use a bathroom, take a photo, or just HAS to have another cigaret. (No intentional air pollution is allowed inside the vehicle.)

If you're in a good-sized city, take the Circle City Tour. Same kind of frolic as around an island.

Some trips offer helicopter rides, windjammer and other boat excursions, horse, burro or llama rides, trips up mountains, down into caves, through historic buildings, museums and flower gardens, and into the air on a parasail. My advice is: Do it all! Or at least as much as your fitness and fears will allow.

If you insist all you want to do on your vacation is relax, take a cruise. You can skip all the stuff they've got going and just lie around, observe the ocean, and listen to your inner self as it converts food into fat.

If THAT's too much for you, stay home and sit on the porch. Saves money.

Strange People

Maybe you're the way I once was--I disliked small talk and felt that conversing with strangers was mostly unproductive. But when you're on a trip, intermixing with people you don't know is great fun.

You develop a delightful camaraderie with the folks traveling on the same bus or ship with you. It's like being a schoolkid again and you're all buddies in the same class.

If letting your hair down and behaving as goofy as you please should cause you any embarrassment later, don't give it a second thought. After your trip you won't have to ever see any of those people again.

4. Going Home

Your last step in the roaming game is Going Home, and it too is a pleasing part of traveling. Although you probably hate to end the trip just yet, when you reach home it feels just GREAT to be back.

You're free to go to the cupboard or fridge at any time. You don't have to carry your dirty underwear around with you but can put it in the hamper. You can reach for a scissors or a pencil automatically and not have to recollect where you keep them.

You can walk around barefoot, telephone a friend, watch television, play with your computer. Being home is WONDERFUL.

Sooner or later, though, you begin to get used to it all. You even begin to get tired of it all. Then one day you notice signs in store windows "Fly to Tahiti!" "Cruise to the Bahamas!" The signs remind you of your travel agent friend, so you decide to stop in just to say "Hi, how are ya."

But WATCH OUT! You forgot about the siren call of the brochure display! Didn't I tell you to beware of brochures?

Then again, if you really want to travel anew and can do it, go to it!

How to Lose Your Favorite Revulsion

Do you ever hear yourself yelling something like:

"Come here and kill this huge bug before it gets away!"

"Get that hamster away from me! I don't CARE if it doesn't bite!"

"If you let your parakeet out of his cage when I'm here, I'll never visit you again!"

"If that cat looks at me, I'm outta here!"

Maybe you have a revulsion--you really hate or fear or get crawly being near some creature that's essentially harmless.

A lot of people have at least one pet revulsion. (That's something like a pet peeve.) If YOU do, you may think it's an inborn, natural trait. You might even feel a secret pride in it because it shows what a sensitive person you are.

My lifelong revulsion was spiders. With vile feelings toward them bordering on the pathological, I felt not squeamishness, but near horror at the sight of a spider, especially a BIG one (quarter-inch or more).

As a teen I even wrote a poem about them:

TO THE SPIDER

Oh, little sick'ning creature with hairy, arch-ed legs,
    How I hate you!
Oh, ugly, morbid spider, (perhaps for life he begs)
    I will grate you!
You seem to symbolize war and gloom, disgusting thing.
    Why are you here?

28

Stay still as I come close; don't move those legs, Outhouse King!
    I have such fear!
This ragged-crawling animal sends loathing through my brain.
    You I must kill!
I feel sick; and though you're dead--a blob where life had lain--
    I hate you still!

During my early married years I'd sometimes "see" in the middle of the night a big black spider on the headboard. I'd shriek and jump out of bed, sending my shocked husband out the other side. Then he'd grab me before I could run out the door, show me there was nothing on the bed and explain that, even if there HAD been a spider, I couldn't have seen it in the dark.

I might have gone on forever spooked by spiders, but luckily I found the root of my feeling and uprooted it.

One day I took my kids to my mom's for a visit. I was standing in her kitchen, when she looked at me and made a loud sickened OHHH! My back and scalp crawled as she rushed past me and smashed her slipper on the wall behind me.

Of course she had attacked a spider, and in a way that made me feel she'd probably saved my life. Immediately I realized that this scene must have happened before, when I was a little kid. Without even a lingering doubt, I knew this reaction of hers long ago was what had caused my horror of spiders.

Somehow, as simplistic as this certainly seems, realizing how my repugnance had been induced made it go away. Since that very time I no longer hate, fear or can't stand being around spiders. Best of all, I no longer have hallucinatory nightmares about them.

If you're plagued with a revulsion, realize it wasn't your idea originally. Somewhere along the way, a person or an event drove it into your little-kid subconscious.

Digging around in your memories and recalling the origin of your revulsion might get rid of it--although you may not obtain an authentic re-enactment the way I did!

Although I still climb up on furniture to terminate any spiders beyond my arm's reach, my heart isn't in it. I feel toward spiders the way most people presumably feel toward ants: we might kill and remove them, but without any real emotion and only in a house-cleaning gesture.

But no one had better test me by dropping a spider into my lap when I'm not expecting it. Although my abnormal UGH is gone, my natural EEEK still persists!

Inventor Go Home

Inventors are going wild with ideas for improving and embellishing the workplace, such as smarter computers in the office, more elaborate machinery in the factory, and more marvelous contraptions to send into outer space. But they're really lying down on the job when it comes to improving everyday life in the home.

The average human being is much more interested in his home life than in his workplace life. At work you do what you HAVE to; at home you do what you WANT to. At least, that's the ideal we're all striving for. But too much of the time you have to toil at home more than would be necessary if the inventors were on their toes.

To give them their due, though, I must mention the delightful creations we already have--the ones that impress me, at any rate:

telephones that answer themselves and take messages,

furnaces that are so smart they sense when it's getting chilly and start themselves up,

nervous yard lights that come on when something gets near them, supposedly startling the wits out of a trespasser; or indoor ones that go on when they sense darkness, even though "darkness" is not an entity,

machines that wash, rinse, and spin-dry dirty laundry, then turn off and sit smugly awaiting praise,

devices that activate themselves and record TV programs from a turned-off television set, (how DO they do that?)

refrigerators that defrost themselves, (although they continually complain about it by pinging, thumping and whirring),

small round ceiling gadgets that blast you and all the neighbors on the street awake if they sniff smoke.

I'm sure you're well aware of these innovations and hardly marvel over them. But I can't TELL you how happy these things make me! That's because I can remember the olden days when . . .

You had to squeeze wet laundry through a rubber WRINGER to get out the excess water. The wringer loved to break buttons in half, and would eat your fingers if you inadvertently made a sandwich of them between two pieces of material.

(There was also a persistent story of a woman who didn't wear a bra and got something quite personal caught in the wringer. But I think it may have just been a legend, because EVERYONE had heard about it but no one ever knew her name.)

Instead of pitching an armload of laundry into a dryer, you used wooden clothes pins to hang up each individual sheet, sock, tablecloth, hanky and stained underwear on a rope strung up in your yard, for any passersby to contemplate.

In the winter you had to dodge around these things hanging in your face in the kitchen. No, not hung in the basement--the basement was a CELLAR, a place you didn't go down into if you didn't absolutely have to. Darkness, dankness, moldy odor, mice, spiders and webs, a place good only for propping up the house and generating Halloween ideas.

I don't recall rubbing dry sticks together to start a fire in a cave, but I do remember a big truck noisily dumping a heap of coal into a hole under the house. (The coal was to be burned in the furnace for heat, if you were wondering. I personally don't know how anyone was ever able to get a piece of coal to burn.)

The pictures you took of people and places weren't in living sound and action. They were dull rectangles that lay silently in bureau drawers, futilely waiting to be put into albums.

Every so often, my mother had to let a large man carrying an ice pick into the house to put an iceberg into our icebox. Her job was to let the ice melt down into a container on the floor and empty it when it began to overflow.

Oddly, when I grew up, I had to toil harder than she did. Although my icebox was electrically cooled, I had to spend hours chipping away ice to defrost the sonofabitch. Now I have a frost-free refrigerator, which I no longer call a sonofabitch but still call an icebox.

I can remember when you had to operate a phone by wearing out your finger spinning a DIAL, and write down your own phone messages with a pencil that always magically disappeared just as the phone rang.

Remembering with distaste days gone by, then, I'm an avid user and appreciator of modern innovations. They give me so much free time, I can spend part of it ambling around the house thinking up further modernizations that haven't been made but certainly should be.

Try to bear with me on this one:

At weddings, showers, and birthday parties, you usually have an overabundance of food, and you've surely learned the time-honored custom of taking at least a taste of everything in sight. (A "taste" is three tablespoonfuls.)

When you literally can't eat another bite, out comes a beautifully decorated cake to a chorus of OOH's and AAH's, stifled burps, and unspoken "yucks".

Of course your host refuses to be stuck with having to eat all that cake, so out next comes the plastic wrap and paper plates, the host insisting that everyone fix up a plateful and take it home to the spouse and the kids.

(You'd think that I, having been a housewife for so many years, would know how to wrap a piece of cake to take home. But without the aid of some rubber bands and a third hand, I'm helpless. I wait till I can nonchalantly pick up a piece someone else has wrapped. If it falls apart in the car, it won't be MY fault.)

So, amid a lot of milling around and friendly banter, everyone eventually gets some cake and takes leave.

Finally arriving at the POINT of all this, commercial bakers take note: bake cakes in 32 (or whatever) piece-size sections, ice each piece, and pack each piece in a little lidded plastic container, 32 of which neatly fit together in a large box with a beautiful frosting-decorated lid.

Now, isn't that better? Everyone who hates screwing around wrapping cake to take home will love you for this. This makes passing out cake a piece o' cake!

Here are some more nifty ideas, which I offer free to any inventor alert enough to make use of them:

A rug whose nap stands itself up again where people leave flattened footprints on it. (Maybe treat it with hair mousse, which does a fine job of standing HAIR up.)

A cupboard that differentiates the older packages and cans from the new, and conveys the new stuff to the rear and the old to the front. To thwart hoarders, it allows only 3 of the same thing in the cupboard, then relentlessly ejects any extras.

Freezer wrap that turns purple when the food inside is about to lose its last drop of moisture, so you'll know you have to cook it today or throw it out tomorrow.

A window screen that, when fingers or toys are poked through it, HEALS when the foreign object has been removed.

Wallpaper containing insecticide. Bugs would automatically die when they crawl on it and drop right off from gravity. This would prevent phobic people in the home from having to make crushed-bug smears on the walls and ceilings. They could simply gather up the wee corpses with a vacuum sweeper.

Toothpaste with a sardine-can-type key at the bottom to neatly roll the toothpaste tube into emptiness. Sorely needed by people wed to a spouse who won't allow a new toothpaste to be opened as long as there's a molecule of paste left in the old one.

To prevent people from using the last sheet of toilet paper, pretending they don't notice it's on empty, and leaving it for someone ELSE to restock: toilet paper that starts a loud annoying signal when the roll nears its end, so that you're forced to change to a new roll just to shut it up.

A device that gathers the crumbs, onion skins, and dried milk patches that eternally collect in the bottom of refrigerators, and flushes them away.

And, to get rid of the thankless and unending job of picking leaves and trash out of the gutters strung around your roof, gutters that have peristaltic action to keep THEMSELVES emptied.

Get on the ball, inventors!

How to be a Superb Grandparent

First, have a child who grows up and has a child. Now you're a grandparent, even though you're much too young and, especially, too young looking to be a grandparent.

When the grandchild reaches the age of speaking, forget all personal vanity such as imagining you're young looking for your age. You will be asked things like "Grampa, what are those wrinkles under your neck?" Tell the little dear they're 'laugh lines.'

"Gramma, how come you have gray hair right on top of your head but not on the rest of it?" Just tell the truth. "Oh, I've been getting lazy about coloring my hair lately."

"How come you color your hair?"

"I don't like having gray hair, so I color it the way I like it to be."

"Boy, I don't like gray hair either. It's UGLY."

"Thank you, sweetheart."

(They'll probably reply, "You welcome.")

"How old are you, Gramma?"

Whisper it to them. Just about any number you say will elicit the same response: "Ohh, that's OLD." (I still can't understand how a 4-year-old knows what's old and what isn't.)

This may sound like a strange rule, but always brush your teeth before you interact with the little ones. Being honest and open, they're going to inform you if your breath is bad. Don't feel insulted--their being shorter than you gives the poor little kids the full effect of your breath when you talk to them. Especially you don't want to offend them when they're on your lap, and feel their heels meet your shins in their sudden effort to escape to fresh air.

Let your grandchildren handle you. I mean like, for instance:

I stood amidst a large group of people in a cheese factory, facing a tour guide who was giving an amusing lecture on the history of cheesemaking. No. 3 Granddaughter stood with her back to the speaker, facing me and playing with the veins on the backs of my hands, completely absorbed in pressing them flat and watching them swell out again.

Just like my kids used to do to my mom, my grandchildren do to me--they like to sit beside me, as close as they can squeeze, and twiddle a mole-like skin tag I have in the bend of my arm. All grandparents have built-in child amusers on their arms. Any kind of a little blotch or tattoo a small child can examine and play with will do.

Little children are also interested in bosoms, the same as everyone else. You don't have to say anything if a grandchild, boy or girl, reaches up and touches the part of Grandma's blouse that's sticking out.

Just don't do as I did once, when one little tyke unexpectedly tried to stick her hands into the two pockets sewn on either side of my blouse you know where, and I giggled and pulled away. This brought on an immediate attack of THREE little grabbers trying to make Grandma giggle some more. I nearly lost my pockets that day.

If you're a man, make sure your grandchildren have the amazing if scratchy experience of rubbing their hands the wrong way on your whiskers. Tell them if they're good little children and eat the crusts on their bread, they'll have whiskers someday too. Tell any granddaughters that you're only kidding.

Any odd talent you have, like wiggling your ears, bending your fingers the wrong way, whistling through a blade of grass, talking without moving your lips, demonstrate to them. This will hugely impress them and provide them with a role model for witless things to practice on a rainy day.

Speaking of role models, if you still smoke, don't do it around your grandchildren. That's one witless thing you don't want them to practice ANY day.

Grandchildren are always leaning against you, stepping on or tripping over your feet (they just can't seem to remember you have FEET down there), climbing up onto your lap, undoing your wristwatch, and combing your hair into a mess. This is why I enjoy being a grandma better than just about anything else. Also because time and again, right out of the blue, they tell you they love you.

Another endearing grandchild trait is their approval of your favorite anecdotes of your past. Unlike your spouse, your children and your best friends, your grandkids LIKE to hear your same stories over and over again.

No matter how young they are, pay attention to your grandchildren the way you would pay attention to a respected and interesting adult. When they speak, look at them and listen. Sometimes they'll say such intelligent and cute things, you'll want to jot them down to tell your friends about. One little guy saw my 2-tooth bridge and said "Those are Gramma's PRETEND teeth."

Once I warned one of them, "Be careful, or you'll fall on your butt!" The child's eyes grew big. "Ooh, Gramma, you said the B word!"

Sometimes they'll ask you philosophical questions and you'll be only too glad to tell them your well-thought-out ideas about schoolwork, Mother Nature, the meaning of life, and the location of Heaven.

Other times they'll say things like "You know what, Grampa?" four times in a row while you're talking to someone else, until you're finally able to answer them, "No, Honey. What?"

"An inchworm bird really ISN'T!"

Here you smile and make a little snort sound in the back of your nose, the same way you do when an adult says something chirpy and unfathomable and you don't feel like asking for an explanation because it probably isn't worth it.

Refuse to have a favorite grandchild. (I personally find this rule impossible to follow, because each one of them is my favorite.)

Along these lines, don't compare one grandchild with any other. Think about this. Would you enjoy being compared unfavorably to some grandma who loves to cook and sew, while you avoid those chores whenever possible?

Whatever does SHE have to do with YOU? Whatever does liking to cook and sew have to do with ANYTHING? Maybe you type and play the piano better than she does; does she give a hoot? Will it ever MATTER that the two of you are different? Remember this tirade if you're ever tempted to compare kids.

Babysit when you wish to, but never against your will. Obviously, I love my grandchildren, but I tend to get unpleasant butterflies in my stomach when I know a stint of babysitting is approaching. This is probably a flashback to the time when I'd produced seven children in nine years and felt like a trapped rabbit.

Especially don't babysit when you really don't want to, and then complain to your friends that your children take advantage of you. As you should have learned from personal experience and Ann Landers, people can't take advantage of you unless you let them.

If you can manage it, though, once in a while startle your daughter or son by offering to take the grandchildren off their hands for a few hours. An easy way to entertain the little ones is simply bring them home (to your house) and show them old family albums, old games and things in the attic, and Grandma's collection of junk jewelry.

When this palls, play games with them which are inane and repetitious. Little kids eat up inane repetition. If your nerves begin to shred, give the children squirt bottles, with a pail of water for refills, to go outdoors and water the flowers with. When they come to realize that watering the flowers is faster if they just dump the pail onto them, think up some other fun.

Let them help you pull weeds or fill a wastebasket with acorns or sticks from the yard. Grandchildren are good cheap labor as long as you do the chore WITH them. When you quit, they quit, and there's nothing you can bribe them with to keep them going.

Of course, when they get older and learn the value of money, you can offer them CASH to do your yard work. But then it's not such cheap labor anymore, is it.

If you feel you need more ideas for kiddie activities, buy a book on the subject. Remember to read it before you bring the grandchildren over.

I use part of the time my grandchildren are with me by giving them a lunch that's different from the routine peanut butter and jelly sandwiches their unimaginative mother always gives them (which, come to think of it, I always gave HER when she was little.)

Try good stuff like fruit yogurt, and sliced deli turkey breast you let them eat without ruining it by engulfing it in bread. Many kids will eat raw vegetables if they're well peeled and cut up and have dip to dunk them in. And, oddly, they all seem to be quite pleased with canned peaches.

To heck with candy or other junk foods! Hide your junk foods before the kids come. If the grandkids like to conclude a meal at your house with a traditional raid on your cookie jar, have a few graham crackers or other harmless crunchies in there.

Speaking of tradition, anything you do TWICE at your house after the kids are old enough to focus their eyes will have to be done every single time they enter your home.

My first kiddie entertainment for my grandchildren was a plastic bag holding a variety of baby rattles, hollow tub-floating animals, pop-apart pantyhose eggs and miscellaneous odds and ends, which I'd bring out for them each time they came over.

I made the mistake of letting them see where I kept it (in the bottom of a closet). So after they learned to walk, the first thing they'd do on entering our house was run to the closet, drag out the bag and pour out the toys all over the living room.

Then, because they'd rapidly outgrown such baby things, they'd go off to do something else, like play Crazy Eights on the computer. I finally disbanded the bag-o-toys and they don't seem to miss it.

But now they're trying to make playing with the computer a fixated tradition. You know--walk in the door, latch onto Grampa, and drag him straight to the computer before they even get their coats off.

This has come about because the grandfather I'm married to shares the play chores when we have the little kids over. His pleasure is to sit beside them while they do all kinds of things on the computer. This is something I can't stand to do, because I get bored and keep wanting to teach them word processing, and some of them can't even read yet.

So while he's watching one of them compute, I take the other ones outdoors to blow bubbles and play hide-and-go-seek, which he doesn't delight in because he's edgy about them possibly harming our bushes when they crawl through them or the flowers if they should dribble bubble liquid on them. (Can you guess which one of us is the real granny around here?)

41

If you think you can ever spend a quiet, peaceful day reading stories to the little children, you must have forgotten all you learned in your parenting phase.

If you try to read them stories any time other than bedtime, there will come an eruption point, when they suddenly jump, run, scream, act silly to the point of lunacy, and try to take the house apart. That's normal healthy energy needing exercise. Obviously you must tire them out before you can achieve any quietude.

Some sure-fire amusements with exhaustion the goal:

Singing fun songs like "Old MacDonald," "Pop Goes The Weasel," "Sing a Song of Sixpence" and other oldies, the louder the better and accompanied by boisterous gestures.

Dancing to the music of your own teen-age records. They'll enjoy your music because it's YOURS, but don't think the kids are going to let you just sit there and reminisce. They'll likely dance only as long as you actively participate, though they won't object if you perform with low-grade agility.

When my kids used to visit my mom, she'd "entertain" them the whole time and spoil them for me, because then they wanted ME to entertain them when they got back home. Being a full-time mother, my constant objective was to get my kids AWAY from me and entertaining themselves.

Well, now I'm old enough to understand why my mom did what she did. When my grandchildren are with me, there are three inescapable reasons why it's impossible for me to do anything BUT entertain and play with them:

1. I realize that someday fairly soon they'll be more interested in doing things with their friends than in doing anything with me.

2. I don't want them to suddenly erupt and take my house apart.

3. They utterly refuse to LET me ignore them to do my own thing. Since I allow them to literally climb all over me, they're not shy about pulling my hand out of my wrist to get me to "COME ON, Gramma!" Just TRY working a crossword puzzle under these conditions.

When the grandchildren become tired and cranky, or the grand-parents become tired and cranky, call the parents and tell them everyone had a good time but all good things must come to an end-- and this is it. (I usually don't set a specific time to end the fun, because I never know how long I can stand to enjoy so much fun.)

If the parents don't answer the phone and mental depletion is setting in, place everyone in front of the television and play a cartoon videotape, an absolutely indispensable commodity for a grandparent. (Also indispensable is a VCR to play it on.)

Sooner or later the parents will answer the phone and you can take their children home. Make an effort of will to ignore the children's pathetic whimpering pleas to stay longer.

Which neatly leads to my next rule: Learn how to say no to your grandchildren. This is a hard one. If one of mine would say, "Dear Gramma, show me how you can jump off the roof," I'd smile indulgently and head out the door for the ladder. This was early on in my grandmotherhood. I have since learned to remain adult and love them thoroughly without being a complete ass about it.

Do not overbuy for them. You don't want them to grow up thinking love is something that comes in a box wrapped with pretty paper and a bow. Besides, when the little ones are feeding you make-believe food on toy dishes in their room, do you ever look around and realize that a time is coming soon when their parents will need to add a couple more rooms onto the house just to hold all the kids' toys, games, junk, and electronic appliances?

Of course, arts & crafts, real musical instruments and books are a different matter. No child ever had too many crayons, pianos or story books.

The last rule is Don't miss out on an opportunity to be a grandparent. If you have no children, or your children have no children, think of being a PRETEND grandma or grandpa to someone else's little offspring, maybe a relative's or friend's. A child can never have too many grandparents.

And a grandparent can never have too many grandchildren. Who else in your life will ever treat you like you're the most wonderful person God ever invented?

The Telephone Message--Take it or Leave it

If at home or on the job you answer the phone for someone who isn't there, and you're expected to take down an intelligible message; OR if you sometimes call others who aren't there and you must LEAVE a message, this message is for you.

When Calling

Speak your name clearly and SLOWLY, with a silent space between the first and last name. If said quickly, your name can sound like something totally different from what it really is.

During my pre-married days, I've told people "I'm Esther McIntosh," and they responded by being puzzled about Mister McIntosh having such a feminine sounding voice.

Dan DiBlando sounds just like Dandy Blando. Some people rather than giggle and say "Is your name really Dandy?" will simply write Dandy Blando on the answer pad.

And no matter how well known you think your company is, the person who answers may never have heard the name before, unbelievable as this may seem. So enunciate it carefully, too.

Then SPELL your name. Slowly. Don't be in such a hurry!

It's a human peculiarity that if someone gives a message in rat-a-tat style, the other person will write it down the same way. Thus the person who gets the message won't be able to read it.

Also, most people find it difficult to write something down by hearing it rapidly spelled. Especially since F sounds just like S over the phone, and V like B.

(Trying to grasp heard letters and string them together with a pencil can be confusing--something like trying to fathom a house number that's in writing instead of numerals, such as thirty seven ninety four. You have to see 3794 before your brain can comprehend it.)

When seeking a call-back, distinctly articulate your telephone number. Before you hang up, have the person repeat it to you so you'll know they didn't just pretend to take it down. Little kids and lazy husbands do that a lot.

Even if the answerer sounds quite friendly, it doesn't mean she recognizes your voice. Or that if she recalls hearing your voice sometime in the past, then of course she remembers the name that went with it.

Therefore, when someone tells you John isn't there, don't say merely "Well, have him call me," and hang up. You may have a lovely distinctive voice, but without a name, John won't know who called him any more than the amiable answerer did.

If you're told that the person you're calling is already talking on another line with someone else, I know it's a great temptation to ask, "Will they be long?", but don't DO it. The phone person probably won't be able to answer that, because most people don't keep their crystal ball next to the phone.

If you have to speak to someone right this minute, and the person who answers doesn't know where they are or when they'll get back, don't turn nasty. Whether at home or in an office, there are times when the answerer doesn't know those details. Just because you think they SHOULD know, this won't CAUSE them to know if they really DON'T know. Got that?

Of course, in a business setting, the phone person could go and find out about So-and-So. If you don't mind being put on hold for who knows how long while they wander around calling into various office doors "Does anybody know where the hell So-and-So went?".

Don't take it for granted when you call somewhere for the second time that day, the same person will answer.

I've answered a phone and had the caller get peeved at me because I asked for information they insist they already gave me earlier in the day. I wasn't even THERE earlier in the day, thank you. (What makes you think I'M the only person who ever answers this damn phone?)

When Answering

When you answer and it's for someone who isn't there, pick up that pen or pencil and write something. Have the caller recite his name and phone number (and his company's name, if business) for you to scribble down even if this same person has called 3 or 4 times that day.

If the fourth time you take only the name, the person he called is bound to have misplaced the previous three messages and desperately needs the person's phone number again.

If it's someone who unendingly calls your kid or your spouse, write it down every time too, so you can demonstrate to your loved one that THIS PERSON IS A PEST. (See to it they quit calling all the time or I'm gonna get an unlisted number and not tell you what it is.)

I've heard callers say something like, "Well, tell Bobby I called him back. This is Debbie." I think to myself, "Debbie sounds like a close friend; and, since she's returning Bob's call, he must have recently called HER. So he surely knows her number."

Consequently, to save on writing energy, I merely scribble "call Debbie." Except Bob, like most of us, knows five different Debbies, doesn't know which one this was, and is vexed with me because he may never know.

Write down the message RIGHT NOW. Try not to let the caller off the hook until you've got it all written down. If they're in a rush, too bad--if they want their message taken they'll have to give you enough time to do it.

In the middle of writing a message, I've hung up just as someone came by and asked me if I've seen Bill. I say no and then write the name Bill on the message pad. That was NOT the name of the caller, but I forgot what was.

Don't leave anything to memory for any length of time. For instance, at the office, Joan steps away to go to the washroom, and her husband calls. You answer and then hang up (not writing a message), planning to tell Joan to call him when she comes back in two minutes.

Of course, you immediately begin to do something else and when Joan walks by, you don't even see her. Later you'll hear it from her that you didn't give her her husband's important message. (He only calls her 8 or 9 times a day, invariably when she's on the phone, in the washroom, or out to lunch.)

THINK before you blurt, so you don't say things ALMOST right. For instance, "Are you hanging on?" meaning "Are you still holding?" I'm not sure I understand why, but when I've accidentally said that to male callers, they've found it funny and laughed about it right in my ear.

I've also asked callers in an inadvertently baffled voice, as though I couldn't believe my ears, "What's your last name?" Say instead something like, "Will you spell that for me?"

Probably the very most important telephone rule of them all:

Don't assume that the person who sounds exactly like someone you've talked to before really IS that person. Be wary about what you say even when you're sure (well, 99% sure) you recognize a voice.

If you talk real chummy, maybe even make some irritating personal remarks, and it turns out they're not who you thought, it can be mortifying. They may be someone IMPORTANT, and important people may lack a sense of humor. If it's your company's customer you've humiliated yourself with, look out.

When a certain daughter of mine who sounds like me lived at home, her boyfriend sometimes called and gave me a very warm greeting before I stopped him with, "Hey, wait. This is her MOTHER."

Hopefully we'll never have to use telephones that show our face on a tiny TV screen. Because, when calling OR when answering, if you say something really idiotic and haven't yet identified yourself, you can quickly say "Sorry, wrong number!" and hang up.

If you happen to get that person on the phone again later, remember to alter your voice and pretend the buffoon they talked to before wasn't you.

How to Survive Riding the Bus

Taking a bus to work or school isn't a whole lot of fun, and can be a strain on a cheerful disposition. If you're one of the many obliged to endure it, here's a survival guide based on 15 years' revealing experience.

Buses You May Meet

I don't know about your city, but in our city we have a huge variety of buses, not one of which is acceptable in all respects.

Some of the buses have windows that were designed permanently closed, even though in hot weather the air conditioning often doesn't work.

Other buses, of course, have windows that will open if you have a good strong arm and don't mind struggling with a stubborn window in full view of an audience.

On the rare bus where the air conditioning still functions, there's always a dummy who opens his window to let in a breeze--a hot, humid one.

On hot buses with no air conditioning but with openable windows, there's always some woman who can't stand having anyone open a window because her hair might get ruffled. You can tell, because she scowls and plasters both hands against the sides of her head as though trying to prevent her hair from sailing out into the street.

Some windows can't be completely closed, and they gradually slide partway open from the motion of the bus. So, in winter, although you tussle uselessly to make the window stay shut, you often acquire an ice cold draft playfully blowing into your ear and caressing the back of your neck.

Sometimes the winter wind whistles in through a window that's actually flapping. I can only figure someone must have read "In case of emergency, lift here" and done just that for no good reason. And nobody has yet seen fit to reconnect it.

On some of our newer buses, when it rains outside it rains INSIDE, dripping from the seam where the wall meets the roof of the bus. If there are no dry seats to escape to, you can hold up a newspaper for protection or just sit there feeling like a jackass, soaking up water until you reach your stop.

There was also one particular bus that utterly reeked of stale urine. Don't buses get hosed down once in a while?

Most seats on buses face front, but there are also some seats that face each other across the aisle. Sitting on one of these, you get the silly feeling that the people facing you are staring at you. You begin to wonder if they're admiring your nice appearance or if they're thinking how homely or fat you look.

You, of course, try not to stare at them because you don't want to give the impression you're admiring or disapproving of THEM. Directing your gaze out the window behind them doesn't help, because you still feel that their eyes are fastened on you or maybe they suspect you're watching them.

If possible, it's hugely preferable to sit someplace where you don't have to be face to face with strangers and imagine foolish things all the way home.

People You May Meet On The Bus

The person (often a large man) who falls asleep and not so gradually collapses onto your shoulder. He needs a pillow, and tag--you're It.

The woman who carries a large loaded totebag strapped over her shoulder and under her arm and has completely forgotten about it. Obliviously, she bonks everyone's head with it as she goes down the aisle. She only remembers the bag when she tries to sit down and the bag, knocking into you, prevents her from getting all the way onto the seat. Then she wiggles and twists trying to disconnect from it while you sit there wondering irritably why she had to pick you to sit next to.

The person who talks to you like a long-lost friend even though you don't know him, can't understand him, and have no remote interest in what he's going on about. But it's hard not to be polite to a person like this, so you sometimes find yourself sucked into nitwit conversations.

The man who hurries to get off the crowded bus and unknowingly drags his jacket over the heads of everyone sitting next to the aisle. Speak of getting your hair mussed! Like a row of human dominoes, a whole line of people hastily lean over their seatmates as they try to dodge the jacket.

The apple eater. You'll never realize how disgusting someone eating an apple sounds until a seatmate does it right next to your captive ear. Ditto the gum chewer-snapper. A gum chomper is one of the few human beings I feel I could abolish. At the very least I yearn to yell "I'll teach you some manners!", stick my hand into her mouth, snatch out the gum and string it through her hair.

The obnoxious stoned person. When you see him stagger up into the bus, pray he doesn't sit next to you. If it looks like your prayer isn't going to be answered, try to sneak away before he gets to you. Go stand near the bus driver or by some other strong looking, hopefully sober, person you imagine might protect you until you reach your stop.

The rowdy teenagers. Teenagers don't ride alone. It's always more than one riding together. They can unnerve you too, but pretend you don't notice them and they probably won't notice you.

If their clothing or hairdos are weird or obscene, pretend you don't see a thing. If their language curls your hair, pretend you don't hear a thing. If they sit behind you and kick your seat or drop cigaret ashes onto your back, pretend you don't feel a thing. Keep in mind that they're just having fun, like you did when you were their age.

The nervous-habit person. On nearly every bus is a "dry sniffer." He sniffs loudly and continually but, you can tell, unnecessarily. (A necessary sniff is one that sounds as though if it isn't sniffed, snot is going to run down an upper lip.) The dry sniffer is intensely annoying, but you can try to be sympathetic with a person who has a nervous habit like that--at least he isn't a gum popper.

The "WET sniffer" is someone who seems to have forgotten his tissues or handkerchief even though he desperately needs them. During winter months there are usually several wet sniffers on every bus. Repress the desire to walk around and supply them all with tissues.

Another tic-ridden person will clear her throat a-HEM over and over, with a variety of inflections and singing styles, until you can't stand it any longer and begin to hope her throat will give out on her. You imagine that if you ahem loudly at HER, she'll realize she's doing it and stop. Well, don't bother. You'll just get a sore throat along with the fit of high blood pressure her unremitting aheming has caused you.

The big-mouth. Some people find their own talk so fascinating they want to share it with the entire bus. It's truly amazing that they don't even have to pause to breathe. It's as though they're lecturing into a telephone, because usually you don't hear any response from the person they're talking to. God help you all if you get two on the same bus in competition with each other. Regular bus riders refer to this as "dueling motormouths."

The seat-hog. Either you're jammed against the wall till your arm falls asleep and you break out in claustrophobia, or you're forced to sit on one-and-a-half hips while one leg and foot hang out in the aisle, in danger of being high-heeled to death. (Believe ME, that's excruciating.)

Bus Drivers You May Meet

The driver who drives like a maniac, who chucks you forward out of your seat at every stop and hurls you down the aisle when you try to reach the door.

The driver who lets you out face to face with a mailbox, telephone pole, high snowbank or deep puddle. Possible reasons for this are that he's mean, stupid, can't see well, doesn't give a damn, or is compulsive about halting the bus exactly at the bus stop, come Hell or deep water.

The driver who keeps letting more people on and saying monotonously, "Step to the rear of the bus, please," even though the bus is completely full, there's no more place to step to, and people are clinging half in and half out the front door.

Various Bus Equipment You Will Meet

The Bell

In each bus there's either a cord tacked up all around, or vertical strips between windows. The cord you pull down on, the strips you press in on. These actions cause a ding up front that signals the driver.

One ding means someone wants the bus to halt at the next stop and let him out. Three or four dings mean the bus driver has zipped past someone's stop and that someone is angry. Dings that go on and on forever cause you to look around to discover who's being so impatient, and then realize all that dinging just means the system is acting up.

All systems on buses "act up." This is why you'll see cords strung on buses along with the original ding strips. The strips no longer work. Something that breaks that readily must not have been any good in the first place, I always say.

The Ticket/Money Taking Machine

This innovation is really great. It sucks the fare right in and, if it's coins, counts it for the driver. No more cheating by riders dumping in a handful of small change that the human driver used to have no way of counting.

Except riders sometimes spend prolonged moments holding up the line while they struggle to insert a bill or ticket so it actually goes into the slot and doesn't simply bend. Of course the machine, being another wonderful modern invention like the ding strips, acts up now and again. Then you're treated to a free ride when the machine stubbornly refuses to accept your money.

The Horn

The fact that the bus is so big and the horn is so loud makes you feel safer riding in the bus than down among the traffic in your much smaller car.

But one morning the bus horn got stuck. At first we thought the driver was having a temper tantrum, but then we saw he was trying to STOP the horn. So the bus sailed on to town blaring full-blast all the way. At each bus stop, the potential riders seemed apprehensive and had to be coaxed to get on.

Seats

Some seats have lost their springs, and when you sit on the cushion you find you're two feet lower than your seatmate. It's embarrassing to appear as though you're sitting in a hole, and it's hard on your butt, but at least it's a seat. Try STANDING when you're being flung around like a rag doll.

Doors

Down through the years people have gotten so used to the doors swinging open for them, they stand and stare blankly at the occasional one that says "When green light comes on, push on door to open." It isn't that we can't read it or don't understand it-- creatures of habit that we are, we just don't SEE it.

And of course the people still sitting have nothing better to do than to yell in chorus "PUSH on it!" Then when THEY get up to leave, they too stare blankly at the little green light as they wait for the door to open itself for them.

The Sign on the Front

In days gone by, bus fronts sported a large paper scroll with assorted names of destinations. The driver would wind the roll until the correct name was showing. Then people waiting at bus stops could read from a ways off where the bus was headed and if it was the one they wanted. Simple.

The newest sign system is digital. It can be made to spell out anything alpha-numeric. (You know, letters or numerals--ABC or 123.) Being currently the best and most modern bus sign system, it screws up.

What then does the driver do whose sign shows blippy lines registering random nonsense? He tapes onto the front window a paper sign scribbled with the bus's number.

Like the people who look at the green light but don't really see it, we look up at the huge digital sign and fail to notice the piece of paper stuck to the glass. Then at every stop the driver has to hear "What bus is this?" over and over again from every person waiting along the route.

Why Ride the Bus if it's so Bad?

It saves wear and tear on your car and conserves gasoline.

If you parked your car as near to work as the bus drops you off, you'd have to pay a parking lot 3 or 4 times what the bus ride costs.

The driver battles the snow, the rain, the pavement holes, and the deranged rush hour traffic while you doze or read or watch the scenery go by.

How to Cope

Always carry an umbrella, one without a long metal point. (I don't think they make dangerous ones like that anymore anyway.) Place it, closed, on your lap with the end pointing toward the dozing-off person who seems to be ready to use you as a pillow.

As he slumps over against you, gradually push the umbrella into his side. When he momentarily sits up and away from you, keep a good grip on the umbrella and slowly push it even closer so he'll feel it as soon as he begins to tip over again. Practice this art so you can do it while innocently looking out the window.

It works. Rather than having an umbrella in the ribs, he may fall asleep in the other direction and topple off the seat into the aisle. That should teach him to get his sleep somewhere else than on you.

An umbrella can also be used for its primary purpose of keeping rain off you when it rains on the bus through those expensive but inferior seams.

Always carry a book with you, to open and read with deep concentration if a Talker sits beside you. If they keep right on yacking, and especially if they haven't brushed their teeth in a long while, either gaze out the window and feign complete deafness, or hang your head down into your lap and feign deep sleep. Don't be afraid of being impolite. What are THEY being?

Any time there's someone doing something on the bus you feel you just can't bear any longer, turn and STARE at them, straight on but expressionless. (Don't scowl or snarl or make any stray motions that might be construed as hex signs or the evil-eye.)

The fixed stare can be used indiscriminately on blabbermouths, apple chompers, gum snappers, aHEMers, sniffffers and seat-hogs. It's not to be used on rowdy teenagers, drunks, or anyone who is holding an animated conversation with himself.

Being confined on the bus amid a bunch of irritating people is one of life's most defenseless predicaments. Although the penetrating peer never seems to accomplish a thing, it gives you SOME feeling of power over what's going on around you.

Whatever you do, don't give in to the instinctive urge to jump up and scream "SIT STILL, QUIT YOUR ANIMAL NOISES, BLOW YOUR NOSE, SHUT UP, AND LEAVE ME ALONE!" Just remember there are also several nice respectable types on the bus, so think of them and try to hold out till you get to where you're going.

Besides, you don't want to be known to these people you ride with almost every day as the only person they ever saw the bus driver boot off the bus!

Tips on Buying Toys

Having bought a tonnage of toys for seven children, many nieces and nephews, and several grandchildren, I consider myself an expert on the subject of toy buying. So, chiefly for you who are parents, here's the scoop.

When buying a toy, there are four main ideas to keep in mind: (1) age appropriateness, (2) safety, (3) quality, and (4) whether you can endure having the toy in the house for more than one day. I'm thinking here of drums, crying dolls, pull-along xylophones, buzzing ray guns, and talking bears.

Age Appropriateness

A baby up to about a year-and-a-half has to have all "mouthable" toys, for obvious reasons.

That is, the toys mustn't have tiny accessories attached to them that the child can rip off and try to eat;

they mustn't be dissolvable under drool;

they mustn't conceal little openings he can get his fingers or tongue caught in.

And they shouldn't be small enough for him to stick 'em in his ears or up his nose. He'll surely try to.

So, luckily for the toy buyer, this rules out a whole LOT of things.

Kids between about 1-1/2 and kindergarten want anything they can use to imitate Mommy and Daddy. Toy household objects of all kinds--dishes, pans, phones, mixers, brooms, etc.--they love.

This is pretty easy, isn't it.

After reaching school age they'll want everything they see on TV and in the homes of their friends, especially electronically speaking. This is the stage in life where Mommy probably will have to get a job if she doesn't already have one.

Safety

Safety should be the foremost consideration in any toy or other child amusement. Except there's nothing but stuffed toys with painted-on features that can be considered actually safe.

If a toy is pointy, it'll accidentally get poked into somebody's eye.

If it's played with on the floor, it'll get tripped over and fallen on.

If it's toyed with in the tub, someone tiny will drink used bath water from it.

If it's hard, a child will hurl it through a window or bop someone with it.

If it's soft, it'll get shredded and some child or pet will try to eat it and then gag up their lunch.

So use common sense and avoid the really dangerous things like bows with real arrows, toxic paints, fireworks, glass dolly bottles, things with sharp metal edges, toy appliances with genuine electric plugs, and toyboxes with weighty lids.

Quality

If plunked down in the middle of a toy store and offered a choice, kids will pick out the most trashy, gaudy toys they can find. But that's not hard to do. At least you, the adult, can read the box to find out what remote part of the world the toy was made in, how many batteries it needs, whether it's been approved by any note-worthy group, and how hugely overpriced it is.

If possible, take the toy out of the package and closely examine it to see how it's made. Usually very very breakable, constructed with the kind of plastic that snaps in two with one good twist.

Then there are "in-betweeners", and these too you have to watch out for. Prime example, a typewriter. You can get your little one a PRETEND typewriter (immovable keys, you see), or an in-betweener: one that really types but is a real pain. It sticks, it breaks, it frustrates. (I think tin is even worse than plastic, don't you?)

Wait till the child can at least read, and then get a REAL typewriter. You can get real items on sale that are infinitely superior to the toy that "really works" and, absurd as it seems, they cost about the same.

Other examples of in-betweener toys that really work but may be crappily made are cameras, sewing machines, computers, pianos, and walkie-talkies.

So search high and low for good quality. Then buy whatever you can think of that will keep the child out of your hair for a few hours. That's the real name of the game.

PCs, Not UFOs, are Taking Over the World

The computer is a fantastic invention that first took over the business world in the 1980's and is now beginning rapidly to take over the personal world of home. Even in the office it's called a PERSONAL computer, nicknamed PC.

Often it's a woman to be blamed for this state of affairs, because women are often the ones who become enamored of PC in whatever office they frequent when they discover PC's Wonderful World of WP.

WP is Word Processing, a means to get something worded perfectly before you even print it. A way to change your mind a million times about one page of words and not get criticized for it. Sheer Heaven for the person who writes anything, even grocery lists, birthday invitations, or an occasional letter to someone who lives farther than a local phone call.

With grit and determination, she pesters her husband with her desire for a PC until the guy feels beaten, and succumbs. Then the two of them, all ignorant unawareness, go off to pick out their very own PC. Although he knows nothing about PCs, she thinks SHE does because she's done a little typing on one.

PC stores are ubiquitous. That means "everywhere." When one goes out of business, another springs up like a mushroom somewhere else. The couple enters one, wanders around looking perplexedly at the merchandise, then answers a salesperson's quiz to the best of their present knowledge, which is nil.

They hear questions something like "Do you want a 449 or a 559? Do you prefer an XT, AT or QT? How much memory megabucks do you want? Do you want a hard drive, a soft drive and a tiny drive? Or will two tinies fit your needs? Will you need a game sport?

What printer do you have? Oh, then you'll need to get one. We have twelve kinds of printers, each with a different number of pins. Will you be wanting one with extra fountains? Will you be plotting graphics? Do you two run your own business? No? Just what do you plan to DO with your PC?"

The wife gets embarrassed, because all she can come up with is "I just want to do some word processing. So maybe we need this little one over here that's stupid and doesn't have very much memory." To impress the clerk that she does SO know PC, she adds "I'll keep my documents on floppy diskettes."

With a cost-conscious, stubborn husband running the show, this search for a PC can take weeks, months, even past Christmas. But if the wife gets her way, within days they'll have their forgetful little computer and nearly letter-quality printer in their home, firmly attached to a heavy-duty surge protector and ready to go. Her diminutive plastic file of diskettes will be sitting dormant nearby, awaiting her every word.

Many PC sellers are shrewd. They HAVE to be, to remain in competition in this mouse-eat-mouse business. They take great care to include a "software package" with every computer they sell. In this package, even though the buyers insist they don't care about games, are games.

New PC buyers think they don't want games, because humans have preconceived notions: before they go on a cruise, they think it's just old folks playing shuffleboard on a listing deck. Before they ever play a computer game, they think they're all childish arcade amusements that shoot down alien blips before they can land on your head.

But, although they only want a computer to use as a glorified typewriter, they install the games that came with it just to see what they're like. Then they fool around with them a little while, till they look bewilderedly at the clock and find it's two hours later and they've forgotten to eat.

The game the PC seller sneaked into their home in the package deal might be one of those that's a little world unto itself. You, the prince or princess, can go wherever you want, pick up, carry and use objects, visit strange lands and personages, get killed and bring yourself back to life, slay evil creatures, save good creatures, unlock locked doors, find hidden treasures . . . You get the idea. These are called ADVENTURE games.

Of course there are other kinds of diversions. Do you like the notion of driving race cars on complicated tracks, or flying fighter planes through the sky, and not getting hurt no matter how fast you go or how wild you get? These are available, called ACTION games.

Would you like to draw pictures and paint them (without getting paint in your hair), create instant circles and squares, make the pictures move like cartoons, change colors anywhere in the picture, switch size instantaneously, add patterns, design kaleidoscopes, turn them upside down and inside out? Software like this is called a PAINT program.

Does sound and music fascinate you in any way? You can greatly enhance the sound that comes from a computer's dinky system with a SOUND program. Write your own music and play it back, on a "piano" that changes its voice to organ, flute, guitar, what have you, and can switch rhythm instantly from waltz to march to bossanova.

Record yourself singing songs with your friends and play them back. Type words and hear a "human" voice read them back to you.

For this kind of program you need a couple speakers and an inexpensive microphone to plug into the computer.

Would you like to play chess with a master chessperson who doesn't take all day to make his move? Would you like to play cards with some jovial people and/or animals who shuffle the deck well and always obey the rules? CHESS programs. CARD programs.

At last you've found out why PCs are taking over. A PC is the answer to an adult child's prayer. A TOY you'll never get tired of, because someone is always inventing wonderful new recreations to perform with it!

Although it's often the wife who finagles to get a PC into the home against the husband's better judgment, he's the one who then goes wild and drags her to PC stores at every opportunity to look at software. Software packages have such exciting interesting pictures and descriptions on them! Being in a PC store is like being in a candy store, only now they have more money than when they were kids drooling over the wares.

Who the heck needs a mouse? No one, except it makes a lot of the software funstuff easier to operate and even more fun. Indubitably and inevitably, these two grownups will one day buy a mouse.

Soon they develop a desire for a monitor with a bigger screen, one with all the colors in the world on it, and much MUCH more PC memory so they can use all the wonderful programs they've bought. Rather than recouping some money from the original PC, they decide to keep it when they get the bigger-better one, because nasty fights have been breaking out over whose turn it is to use it.

The only down side to all this is that each new interactive amusement they accumulate first requires them to study the sizeable directions and learn how to use it. That's a bummer, a downer, a real pain in the neck. But they'll do it, if not now then later.

Meanwhile . . .

They find themselves again in another PC store, spying something else that's enticing. Fly a helicopter! Play golf on the moon! Captain a submarine! Learn to write novels, make a million dollars, play arcade games!

Self-mesmerized, they buy a joy stick and a package of adult arcade games, go home and begin shooting down alien blips before they can land on their head.

The end result of getting a little PC for a small amount of WP is an entire room filled with PCs, diskettes flopping all over everything, and so many wires running to and fro, the PC user's afraid to turn on a lamp.

What can you do about it?

Warn your friends!

Most assuredly, don't let it happen to you!

Owing to the whims of sex and Mother Nature, most babies are born at random. Nonetheless, here's a little guide to help you plan how many children you might want if you and your person of other sex have any say in the matter:

ONE CHILD

If you have only one child, be prepared to hear it called an "Only Child" by almost everybody, who seem to imply the tot will be either a spoiled brat or pathetically lonely. The REAL bad news about having just one child is that you'll find yourselves more distressed by its smallest action than you'd be if you had, for example, a Gang (described later).

An only child's every desire takes on an added importance and its every disease an added horror because it's your only one and there are no others to distract you. So you probably should consider

TWO CHILDREN.

A brother or sister for your child is a good idea, because this will give it someone to play with and talk to and follow around besides you--which certainly will be a relief to you.

A sibling will also give your firstborn someone nearby to tease, punch and blame things on, which will be a relief to the previously Only Child.

The major trouble with having two children is that forever after you'll hear two directly opposite stories of what goes on with them when they're out of your view.

If your two children are the same sex, or if they can't stand the sight of each other, you might decide to have

THREE CHILDREN.

Hopefully you will by this time have an opposite-sex child among your little group. If not, well, you can still save money by passing down their clothes.

You'll be much more casual with number 3, because now you'll know how run-of-the-mill most of his fevers and tantrums will turn out to be. And three children ARE enough to distract you.

Many couples judge that three children are the ideal family. But if after having three you're still not satisfied with the sex distribution, or if you just love having a little baby in your arms, you might decide you'd like to have

FOUR CHILDREN.

As one child is invariably called an Only Child, four children are referred to as Plenty.

Four is a good number of children because most recipes serve six--Daddy, Mommy and Them. A half-dozen doughnuts, eggs, or rolls are handy items to serve, unless Picky will eat only a bite of anything and Chubby wants three of everything. (Of course, even that seems like it would work out.)

If you're lucky enough to have two boys and two girls, it'll give you something to brag about, although probably your mom will be the only one actually impressed by this.

If one day by some odd stroke of fate you find that one of you is again expecting, you will have

FIVE CHILDREN.

Now you have a Gang. It's hard to find something fascinating to say about having five children, except that each new baby, besides adding extra diapers and spit-up, brings a cute new face and unexpected new pleasures to the parents.

For instance, maybe number 5 will find toilet training something HE wants to accomplish, unlike the first four who you thought would need diapers packed for them in their lunchboxes when they went to school.

By the time you have five children, even your favorite relatives will sometimes forget your kids' names, confuse their faces, and flagrantly call them your Gang.

When you meet old acquaintances, they'll gape and ask "Are these all yours?" as though your five have suddenly doubled or tripled in number.

If after all this you find you're fanatic about even numbers or are still stubbornly hoping for a child of opposite sex, you may go so far as to have

SIX CHILDREN.

Having six children is nice if you don't mind overhearing your friends, relatives, and even your parents mutter things like "OhmyGod" whenever you and your children come into their view or their living room.

But you'll find you won't want to take all eight of you to very many living rooms anymore because you no longer fit in the car. At the same time, you'll discover it's nearly impossible to unearth a sitter stouthearted enough to watch six kids all at once. So this number of offspring truly generates family togetherness.

In fact, if sometimes you crave to be alone to think your own thoughts for five minutes, you'll have to learn to sneak, and a room with a lockable door will be a necessity. Need I mention that with one child or six you'll never choose the bathroom for your hideout? One of them will notice you're hiding in there and will instantly become frantic to use the potty.

If, as the old but apt cliche goes, you're a glutton for punishment, you just possibly may want to have

SEVEN CHILDREN.

Well, seven IS supposed to be a lucky number. Seven of them plus you and your equally culpable spouse will fit nicely into a nine-passenger station wagon if you can get one.

But even if you CAN all fit into your car, you'll learn there aren't many places you'll WANT to take seven kids all at once. If it hasn't already dawned on you, seven children totally outnumber and outrun you.

Like taking them for a day at the park and then getting them together when lunchtime comes. You send Big Sister off to get Middle Brother. When they forget to return, you send out Big Brother to find the ones you first sent out.

When no one bothers to come back, with dire threats you send another kid to go find all the others. An interminable time later, when they've finally been rounded up, you'll feel much more like rapping on them with your knuckles than feeding them.

Come to think of it, seven is probably beyond the scope of your interest, since it's highly unlikely you and your Loving Other would PLAN to have seven children.

Obviously, what comes next is

EIGHT CHILDREN.

Because I have only seven, I'm not qualified to speak on the various life aspects of having eight. So this is (I HOPE!) the end.

Intro to Word Processing

Q.   What is the ultimate product of word processing?   That is, what are we going to all this trouble FOR?

A.   The end product of all the complex learning necessary to use word processing is the DOCUMENT.

Q.   O.K. So what must I do first?

A.   You must first CREATE the document, a god-like undertaking, and give it a name, a parent-like undertaking. After you have created and named the document, you will want to REVISE.

The first rule of word processing is: DOCUMENTS NEED REVISION. If a document doesn't need revision, it doesn't belong in the computer and you should have nothing to do with it. Now tell the SYSTEM you want to revise.

Q.   What is the SYSTEM?

A.   For the sake of having our own word processing jargon, we call the computer the SYSTEM.

Q.   How do I get the system to bring back a document I've created so I can revise it?

A.   The system will prompt for the document's name. Here's where you cannot fake it. You must use the precise name, or keep offering other names until you hit upon the absolutely correct one. If you never get the name right, that document may be lost for all eternity.

Q. If I can remember the document's name and tell it to the system, what happens?

A. If you finally remember the correct name and offer it to the system, the document will be displayed on the screen in living colors, if your monitor has colors. If your monitor is in monochrome, the document will appear in one ugly color.

Q. Then what?

A. You will then want to get to the point of revision quickly, rapidly, speedily, and hastily. Four ways to do this are by using: Quickness, Rapidity, Speed and Haste.

Also you can use the HOME key to immediately reach the top of the page. Use the PAGE DOWN key to reach the bottom of the page. Use the PAGE UP key to reach the previous page. Use the END key to reach the end of the line. Use the Restroom Key to reach the appropriate bathroom.

Q. What is the correct way to use these keys?

A. Use one, all, or a combination of these keys to reach the revision point without screwing up the text. There is no one correct way. There are many incorrect ways. By intense practice you will uncover all the incorrect ways to do a process or function.

Q. What is the CURSOR? Does it actually CURSE?

A. No. The CURSOR is a little blinking underline that is YOU. Anything else on the screen is part of the document or menu or fingerprints or dirt. So please never forget that the cursor is YOU.

Q. What are those four little black arrows used for?

A. The ARROW KEYS are probably the most important ones on the entire keyboard. They enable you to home in on the exact place you want to position your cursor (yourself) to erase/ DELETE or add/INSERT letters.

Q. What is the BLOCK function?

A. Pressing BLOCK will give you Block information, enabling you to move things, delete things, copy things, or overstrike things. After you indicate which function you need, you **highlight** the area you want to work on. (The Things.)

Block is the most fun function in the entire catalog of word processing, but don't waste a lot of your time fooling around with it.

Q. What if I highlight the wrong things?

A. If you happen to highlight the wrong things, press ESCAPE. Whenever you do something ignorant, foolish, senseless or ridiculous, use the Escape key. It's the second most important key on the keyboard. Learn where it is and make it your friend.

Q.   Please explain SEARCH & REPLACE.

A.   A final method of making major revisions that reduces retyping is using SEARCH & REPLACE. You search for a wastebasket and replace your diskette into it.

Q.   What is just plain SEARCH?

A.   Just plain SEARCH is a function where you push the Search key and the system prompts: "Say What?"

You type the sequence of characters or codes you want to locate. Exactness is imperative. Then press Enter. The cursor will move to the first instance of that code or character string. Then do whatever you want with the string.

Q.   What is the PAGE BREAK function key?

A.   The PAGE BREAK makes a new page appear as if by magic! If you forget to use it, after you've typed a certain number of prearranged lines, a SOFT PAGE break will materialize across your screen. The computer is trying to tell you it's time for a page ending if you don't want your words running off the bottom when they're printed.

Q.   What is the BACKSPACE for?

A.   When you are typing (actually you're keyboarding, but everyone calls it typing) and make a mistake, press BACKSPACE to back up and remove the incorrect character.

Type in the correct character.

Press Backspace again because you have again typed an error.

Then really type in the correct character. OOPS!

Press Backspace to back up and remove the oops.

Q.   How do I use the TAB KEY?

A.   To use the TAB KEY:

Press TAB to reach the tab position you want. Tabs are preset for you every 5 spaces on the scale line.

Keep tabbing over until you get where you want to go or the cursor falls off the right margin of the page and onto your desk.

Q.   How do I change the document's format?

A.   Most format changes can be made in the Line Format menu, the Page Format menu, or the Margins and Tabs menu. There is also a menu that allows you to make specific format changes using all these menus.

Additional menus used for format changes are discussed in the "Creating Headers and Footers" menu. For specific information on formatting, refer to the document format options in the pull-down menu.

When you weary of using these countless menus, consult the lunchroom menu.

Q.   Please explain the SAVE function.

A.   As you type and see the words appear on the screen, you probably think you're creating a document. You are not. You are only placing electronic blips in the computer's MEMORY.

If you leave word processing to use some other function of your computer, or if you turn off the computer, all those reams of scholarly information you just typed disappear into thin air.

So before you even get up to stretch, press SAVE and answer whatever tedious questions the computer then asks you. This will preserve on a disk the document and whatever changes you made in it so you can find it later to re-revise.

Q.   What is the difference between a disk and a diskette?

A.   Nothing. But a HARD disk is the one built inside the computer, and a FLOPPY disk is one you can carry around with you. (If you also happen to carry a magnet around with you, try to remember to keep it in a different pocket.)

Q.   How do I PRINT the document?

A.   When printing a document, the document must be available to the system. If you have stored the document on your fixed disk, it is always available.

If it is stored on a floppy, that diskette must be in the appropriate disk drive so that printing can take place. For some reason, the computer cannot print from a disk that is three feet away in a file box.

Q.   How do I CENTER something?

A.
                          Centering is Here
                  Caused by Pressing Centering Key

Q.   What if I need HELP?

A.   There is a HELP function key. It is thoroughly easy to access, explains everything you could possibly think of to ask about, but is impossible to find a way out of. Use it only as a last resort.

Q.   What's this about a last resort?

A.   The "cold boot" is your ACTUAL last resort. Sometime in the life of every computer comes the second when something you do causes it to "lock up", "freeze", or "die." At that time you can press any and every key and nothing has any effect. The computer placidly sits there and hums at you.

Q. So how do I "cold boot" the system? Do I actually boot it with my foot? Should I take my shoe off first?

A. No. You may have the DESIRE to kick it, but it's not a requisite. Take out any disks that may be in any drive. Then hold down these three keys at one time: CTRL, ALT, DELETE. Let go as your computer blacks out and then starts itself up again, going through its self-mumblings.

When it is functioning anew, you can get back into what you were doing. Just don't do THAT again--whatever it was you did that locked it up in the first place.

Q. But sometimes my fingers take over from me and type things I haven't even decided on yet. Is this normal?

A. You'll find that if you word process a great deal, your fingers often develop a mind of their own and frenziedly press keys they think they should, but not ones that YOU think they should.

Therefore, if you can't figure out what you did wrong that froze the computer, next time just don't finger the keyboard so darned fast!

Q. What use are those other black, green, red and blue words spread all over my keyboard template?

A. Any word processing system worth its great expense has dozens more dazzling functions for you to learn, which we haven't covered here.

You can UNDERLINE and BOLD, MACRO and MERGE, SETUP and SWITCH, SPELL and THESAURUS, COLUMN and MATH, FLUSH RIGHT and FOOTNOTE, LIST and REVEAL!

To learn how to accomplish these fascinating feats, read your Word Processors Manual. Simply use intense concentration to study the endless pages of overwhelming detail until you begin to sob or curse.

Then put down the unwieldy manual and find someone who already knows how, and pick their brains.

How to Prepare a Feast
In Your Own Simple Kitchen

Being a person with a lot on your mind, your first objective is to remember what day it is you're supposed to serve the feast. If it's Christmas, think about it during December. If it's Thanksgiving Day you let your relatives stick you with, mull it over sometime during the last couple weeks of November.

Better look it up on the calendar, because Thanksgiving is one of those roving holidays that lands on a different date every year, like Easter. Easter is still worse, because you won't even know which month it comes in unless you check it out. Try March or April.

Dig out your lifetime accumulation of cookbooks and push aside the ones that are thoroughly yellowed with age, have multiple food stains, or have their pages falling out. Try to find an intact one with a directory in the front or back that gives recipes by meal categories: breakfast, brunch, lunch, dinner, snack, and midnight pig-out. You'll find that cookbooks like these are adequate, though dull.

You might also come across one of those jollier types of cookbooks that feature recipes assembled under holiday categories, including Flag Day, Arbor Day, Earth Day, Fourth of July, and Groundhog Day. These have cute child and teenage type ideas, mainly the food being color-coded to the theme of the day. Everything red for Valentine's Day, all orange and black for Halloween, all green for St. Patrick's, and so on.

After you skim through it and have a few laughs, go back to your everyday cookbooks. But you'll soon notice that if you follow their rules, you'll have to do a lot of COOKING. Who wants to do

THAT at a party or on a holiday? Since modern supermarkets are filled with wholly or partly prepared foodstuffs, and no doubt you have a microwave, home in on quick-fix menu ideas.

Of course a turkey isn't quick to cook, but at least you can use ready-prepared stuffing, instant mashed potatoes, already brown-sugared yams, oven-ready rolls and ready-baked pies. Don't fret over what the guests will think. The people you cook for won't perceive any difference between homemade (pronounced ho-made) and store-made if you've hidden the wrappers. And they won't dare murmur anyway because they'll be afraid they might get stuck with presenting the next feast.

By the way, if you're going to have a sizeable turkey roasting in the oven for several hours on the big day, realize you won't have room to bake anything else in there at the same time. I once had to bake three pies after the turkey was finally done and we were sitting down to eat it, and by the time the pies came out of the oven and cooled, no one was interested anymore.

If your feast is to be for a baby shower, graduation, or some other non-traditional get-together, it'll be harder to plan for because then no one can tell you what you're SUPPOSED to serve. So go ahead and fix foods that you like best. You're the one going to all the trouble.

When you finally decide what to feed the guests, write down the various foodstuffs you need to buy. Then the day before the feast, track down the list and take it to the supermarket, carrying a lot of money with you to buy the ingredients.

When picking out ingredients, stay away from Diet Food selections, because they're all sugar-free, salt-free, fat-free, cholesterol-free, calorie-free, preservative-free and thus nearly ingredient-free. You might get home with something and find it's just a package of air.

After you get back with the groceries and have deposited them in every spare spot in your kitchen, inspect your good dishes. If your last feast was prepared some time before, your good dishes are sure to be covered with a coat of dust and some tiny dead bugs.

You'll be tempted to just wipe them off with a used dish towel, but think how you'd feel if someone fed YOU on wiped-off dishes at a feast. Some of that dust may be dirty, so wash those dishes.

While you're at it, see if you have a big enough platter, sufficient pots and pans for what you're going to cook, enough matching glasses for the number of people coming to the meal, and whatever else you need that never entered your mind until this very day.

Next, climb up on a chair to hunt in the upper cupboards for all the items you couldn't find anywhere else. Hopefully when the chair tips over backwards you'll be able to leap aside without yourself going over with it.

Then make a list of the things you couldn't find but urgently need, and plan to call someone near and dear to bring them to you today or, at the latest, tomorrow morning.

Check out the various appliances you'll be wanting to use, such as the big coffee maker and the blender. See if they're clean and whether they work. If one of them gives you an electric shock, figure out what caused it.

If it wasn't wet hands but was instead a defective cord, search lower cupboards, basement storage boxes, and shelves in the garage for a different cord. If you manage to find one, test it quickly to see if it works without giving you another shock, because the day's moving on and you haven't even begun to cook anything yet.

When you're all set to begin preparing the actual meal, clean the house. Too bad you didn't think to do this yesterday, TWO days before the feast.

To enhance speed, simply PUT EVERYTHING AWAY, not worrying over where the stuff belongs. Then clean only obvious pollution. But don't fuss. You can do real cleaning next week on the mess that'll be left from the party. Most crucial is the icky bathroom and its fixtures, to be scrubbed just before you get into bed later tonight.

After serenely imagining yourself getting the food fixing done the day before the feast, you suddenly realize that most of the cooking will have to be done on the day of it. That's the way life goes in the world of food prep.

It's only when you tiredly flop into bed that you recall it's also too late to spruce up the yard and go to the beauty shop. But what the hey. If you provide lots of food and alcoholic quaffs for these people, no one's going to pay much attention to your yard or hair.

Get up early when the big day arrives, and begin to cook your feast. You want your kids and pets to feel loved and wanted, so let them pass freely through the kitchen during the food fixing. Just remember to constantly remind them to get out of the way, and be ready at all times to give them a hand or an elbow to aid them in doing it.

To save time, leave spices, seasonings, flour, measuring utensils, boxes, bags, bottles and bins out until the whole meal is prepared. Resolve that the next time you move, you'll choose a house with a bigger kitchen and a lot more counter space.

Somehow people always begin arriving before you're ready for anyone. So when you hear people early at the door, have your children let them in so you can hurriedly set the table and continue to watch over whatever is cooking.

(Man-of-the-house is glued to the TV set. He's leaving it up to you to make this party a success, since it wasn't HIS idea, and you're the woman.)

Send the early arrivals to the alcoholic beverage display so they won't be annoyed that the meal isn't ready yet and that the man doesn't seem inclined to entertain them. To be cordial, join them briefly for a couple of quick ones.

When it's nearly time for the actual feast, run upstairs without stumbling and put on dangling jewelry and a fancy dress so you'll appear blase', as though making a huge feast in your own simple kitchen is a commonplace occurrence.

When the food is actually finally ready to serve, carry several dishes at one time to the table to speed up the action and display your dexterity. Have your children and the pets clean up whatever unexpectedly reaches the floor instead of the table.

Don't wait longer than one extra hour for that last couple of relatives who pledged to be there but haven't showed up yet. Then invite everyone to the table to enjoy the feast, even if parts of it have grown cold, dry, hard, or runny during that last hour.

The hardest part of this whole orchestration will be to sit down at the table with your guests and actually eat a few bites of your own food before everyone else is finished and it's already time for you to jump up and:

clear away all the empty plates, sticky silverware and used napkins;

find room in the dishwasher, sink, counter and garbage can for all the dirty dishes and scraps;

find suitable containers, with matching lids, for fifteen kinds of leftovers;

find space in your refrigerator for all those leftover-filled containers; and

remove food fragments from your dangles before they petrify.

* * * * * *

Wasn't that fulfilling?

Aren't you glad you've taken a vow never again to prepare a feast in your own simple kitchen for as long as you live?

Babies, First and Last

Some new parents may argue against this premise, but it's true, regardless: parents treat later babies differently from the way they do the first.

The first baby, no matter how many parent-prep books you read ahead of time, will be a novelty and an experiment. When later babies come along, you'll have had experience and will think you know what you're doing. Then what you do might not be better but it will certainly be different.

What follows refers to you having a first baby and a last baby in a family of more than one baby. Preferably several.

With your firstborn child, you're all prepared with prearranged names; as soon as you know its sex, it will take you no time at all to decide on its name. Thus, baby No. 1: Elizabeth Rosemary.

With the last child, you take days to figure out what to call it, because all your favorite names have been used up. In the hospital they keep pestering you with the birth certificate registration, insisting that you name the child, or at least write down SOMETHING. Thus, Baby Last: Joe.

You dress No. 1 as simply and gently as possible, because you hate upsetting her. When you try to push her skinny arms through her sleeves, her fingers get tangled in the openings; when you try to stuff her big (comparatively speaking) head through a neck hole, she immediately begins to gasp because she thinks she's going to suffocate from the cloth being over her face, till her head pops through.

Thus you mostly stay away from dresses for the first half a year, even though they're so adorable, and attire her in front-opening all-in-ones with handy snaps. Not buttons. You don't want to run the risk of one of the buttons coming off and jumping down her throat when no one's looking.

By the time Baby Last comes along, you have attained a fine efficiency in getting a little one dressed, and have learned not to waste so much TIME at it.

Without even thinking about it, you're able to stuff him into his snowsuit without catching his lips in the zipper, cram his feet into his shoes with most of his toes facing forward, and squirrel his fingers into his gloves with all the fingers in the thumb hole, in short order.

You find that YOUR baby really IS cuter and sweeter than anyone else's baby ever was, and you crave to show her off to everyone you ever knew or had any remote contact with.

So you put a bonnet on her little bald head and cart her to where you used to live, where you used to work, the restaurant you hung around in when you were a teenager, your old supermarket, and to every place else you can think of where there may be someone who'd love to gaze at your child, the darlingest little baby they'll ever see.

With Last Baby, when people ask "Why didn't you bring the BABY for us to see?" you tell them, "You've seen his big sister, haven't you? Well, he looks sorta like her."

You take such pleasure in detailing to everyone every little thing First Baby does--how many ounces she puts down, how she sounds when she sucks, how often she wakes in the night, the variety of her gurgles and what they mean, how she turns up the corners of her mouth when she smiles, how she burps so cutely after she eats.

You begin to notice that your friends have stopped phoning you to chat, and people seem to be trying to avoid you.

When friendly people ask you about Last Baby, you offer the fascinating information that the Little One is already somewhere around 4 or 9 months old.

As to having a baby SLEEPING somewhere in the house, with the firstborn you whisper a lot, annoy yourselves by constantly shushing each other, and keep the telephone and the TV turned down almost to oblivion so as not to disturb the Baby.

With Last Baby, it doesn't dawn on you to turn down your voices or the TV even at midnight just so's not to wake him. If anything, you speak louder and turn UP the TV so you can hear it over the children's noise if any of them happens to still be awake.

You never tire of taking photos of your first baby, from naked to snowsuited, from sleeping to screaming, 15 different shots of her before she even leaves the hospital, and a whole roll on the day she learns to walk.

A few years later, someone will start a rumor that you actually ADOPTED Last Child as a third grader, because no one can find any photos of him when he was little.

Of course you sterilize the nipples that go into Baby's mouth, whether they're rubber ones or Mommy ones. And you always wash a toy or pacifier that touches the floor before you let it touch her again.

By the time of Last Baby, you have grown a bit more blase'. If he drops his pacifier on the floor when you're changing him in the ladies room at the mall, you just pick it up, blow on it, and wedge it back into his mouth.

You and the grandparents, godparents, aunts and uncles of First Baby buy her so many toys, you have to dig down and search for her among all the playthings when it's time to do something with her.

Being rational folks, you wouldn't dream of buying toys for Baby Last, because he already has two roomfuls of serviceable stuff left over from the first babies. On his birthday, you give him a piece of cake, a glop of ice cream, and a new pair of shoes.

The most heart-rending part of being a new parent is having to leave Baby with someone else for the first time, and you nearly can't bear to do it. If you're the Mom, Baby's been in your belly for nine months and in your arms for weeks more, and it seems inconceivable to go where you're not even going to be on the same STREET with her.

Even if you leave her with your mother, mother-in-law or someone else just as completely trustworthy, and you're only going to be gone an hour or two, you provide the caretaker with a written set of instructions. You can't expect her to remember everything, and you don't trust anyone other than yourself to do it right anyway.

The list details the exact time the baby has to be fed, the specific number of ounces of milk and teaspoonfuls of baby food to deposit into her, the number of diaper changes in every half hour, the amount of ointment to put on her bottom at each change, and how to set up the fully equipped baby-bed if she needs a nap.

In the diaper bag is a large container of gooey tissues, several diapers, 6 jars of baby food, 4 bottles of formula, two pacifiers (in case one loses its sterile properties), two bibs, her special spoon, an extra sweater in case the temperature drops, bottom ointment, powder for her delicate neck crease, a rattle, a teething ring, and her favorite stuffed toys, three of them in case she suddenly becomes hard to please.

With Last Baby, you take the first possible opportunity to leave him with a relative or friend, because you're wild to get out of the house after taking care of children all the time.

But you still give instructions: you tell them that when he gets hungry, they can feed him whatever they're going to have. You tell them not to bother to change him if they think it's an annoyance--you can do it when you get back. If he needs a toy, give him a newspaper to shred. And lay him on the floor if he gets sleepy--he rolls off beds.

As is nearly too obvious, Baby Number 1 is dearly loved. As incredible as it may seem, Baby Number Last is dearly loved too, whatever its actual serial number. The only real difference is that down through the years a lot of FEAR and FUSS has gotten discarded along with the bathwater.

How to be a Slumlord or Slumlady

After spending our first married year in a 1½-room apartment with a bed-in-the-wall (called Murphy), my husband and I came up with a bright idea. We took our savings and plunked a down payment onto a two-family house on an old but neat street.

Then we moved into the upstairs of it and rented out the bigger downstairs. Happily for us, the downstairs rent covered our mortgage, and in a few years the house was paid for!

Gosh, we thought, isn't this neat? And weren't we smart? And isn't landlording really the way to go?

Of course, living right over your tenants when you're real young and look even younger than you are is a touchy proposition. Some of them had kids older than I, and when I'd go downstairs to politely ask them to please quit doing whatever it was that sounded like pounding sledge hammers on the walls and killing cats, they wouldn't take me seriously.

Once when the parents weren't home, the kids had what seemed like every child in the neighborhood running through the place, in the front door and out the back, round and round, slamming the doors and screaming. It was senseless mayhem, and made me fear for the property and my nerves.

When the parents got home and my husband came home, I sent him down to speak to them. Being young himself, but tall, dark and mean, my husband got our complaint registered and received oodles of reassurance. Fine, until the next time they left their kids alone.

We tried hard to be thoughtful landlords. My husband even made the minor gaffe one time of asking a woman what color she might like us to paint the living room before she moved in. She said it was nice of him to ask, but she didn't really care what color as long as it wasn't chartreuse. She hated chartreuse.

I don't remember what color paint we used, but when the woman moved in she brought a three-piece living room set of the definitely chartreuse persuasion.

That's when we began to learn not to believe everything people say, especially ones who try to convince you that they're really NICE, ready to respect your property as no other renter you ever had, and intend to actually pay the rent every month if you'll let them move in.

When this house was paid off, we used it as a down payment on a single home, because we were tired of being live-over landlords. But Time is a great trickster. Soon we forgot all the bad parts and remembered only the good parts--namely, THE RENTERS PAY THE MORTGAGE.

So, again feeling we were being clever, we put a small down payment on an old two-family house in a neighborhood on the other side of town. We lived in our single house, and got TWO rents from the double.

We figured that whatever the renters would do, we wouldn't be within sight or sound. The ones downstairs could tell off the ones upstairs, and vice versa. They could police each other, so to speak, and we could stay out of it. Simply go over there once a month and collect the money.

At this point, you must be eager to hear how you too can prosper by getting rental property and letting THE RENTERS PAY THE MORTGAGE.

Speaking mainly to those who must start out the way we did, with only a small amount of money to put the process in motion, I'm delighted to offer you my advice on how to attain this worthy goal.

Find yourself a sturdy house, most preferably a two-family, in an old but polite neighborhood. Put the tiniest down payment on it that you can get away with. Obviously, when this house is paid off, it can be the down payment on a FOUR-family. See how that works? (You can envision it as being like an upside-down pyramid with you trying to balance on top.)

To entice renters, partly or fully furnish the rooms with your old furniture, curtains, etc. This is a keen way to make use of out-moded things you were keeping because they were too good to throw away.

Mention the furnishings in a pleasant but wordy manner when your tenants first move in, this way broadly hinting that you expect to find the stuff still there when they leave.

About gas, electricity and water bills, always let your tenants pay their own. If YOU pay their utilities, any possible profits will flow out the window, up the chimney, and down the drain.

About cockroaches, also let them furnish their own.

I've been a renter myself, so I don't mean to sound snotty, but renters can be like little witless kids. For example, they may not realize that flushing diapers, wooden clothes-pins and toys down the toilet can potentially obstruct the water opening.

Or that a potful of bacon grease might do something unpleasant to the kitchen sink drain.

Or that when a window gets broken (to their complete astonishment and innocence), it wasn't you, the owner, who did it just for the fun of having to travel crosstown to dig out the old shards and cram in a new pane before rain and pigeons take this opportunity to get in and ruin the place.

Don't be hesitant about giving your tenants your telephone number, whether or not they have their own phone. They've got to be able to call you about important matters, such as:

they're holding the rent for you if you can dash over before they have to leave for work--if not, you can try to catch them home tomorrow or next week,

a fuse blew,

a faucet's dripping,

they saw a spider in the basement,

they moved out last week and they wanted you to know so you won't come looking for last week's payment,

there's a fire in a wall and they don't know how to put it out.

Tenants tend to look up to The Owner as if to some kind of a parent figure, seeming to take literally the label of landLORD. When the Other Tenants do nasty things anytime day or night, they'll keep you informed by phone and expect you to come and holler at them.

Of course, the Other Tenants will call you and tell you all the unneighborly activities of the first tenants. Both groups will expect you to take sides. I can only advise you not to totally take seriously anything any of them tells you unless the police are involved.

For some reason, many renters have nothing but bad luck, BAD luck. Someone is always stealing their welfare check. Even if it's been direct deposited! Now I call that Bad Luck with a capital BL.

Oftentimes there's an ex-husband who won't send his child-support check to your tenant on time so she can pay her rent in the punctual manner she promised. She may tell you he's a vile insect, but the Other Tenants will inform you he stays there overnight many a night and it's not to pick a fight.

It's terrible too how your tenants are forever getting taken advantage of. Willy-nilly they're always getting hired and then fired and not paid. They also do a lot of odd jobs for people who refuse to pay them with money but only with beer, cigarettes and pet food.

At every turn they're cheated and tricked and bad-lucked out of the rent money. And it's never their fault, so you can't blame THEM.

To act like a real landlord, you must make a few rules, even though there's no way in hell you'll be able to enforce them. We were firm about not renting to people who had any more than four children. Seeing that their half of the house had only two small bedrooms, we thought we were being eminently reasonable.

No tenants ever had more than four children before they moved in; then they did constant babysitting, so the extra kids and babies staying there weren't really theirs.

We didn't even TRY to prohibit pets. Rumor has it there's some kind of a law requiring that, the lower people are on the rent scale, the more cigarets they must smoke and the more animals they must keep. (Pets, not ex-husbands.) I'm quite skeptical that there is such a law, but a lot of our tenants seemed to believe in it.

The first thing to think of when hearing the word "tenant" is TEMPORARY. Some of them will be clean and quiet and pay the rent on time and never bother you, but they too will fly the coop when you're least expecting it. But, luckily, all these people fast-forwarding through your rental property will have a relative or acquaintance looking for a place to run up a rent bill in.

Enjoy it or not, you've got to keep an eye on what goes on at your property if you don't want the entire place to disappear off the face of the earth sometime when you've forgotten to check up on it for a couple of weeks. To do this there are sneaky practices you're going to have to learn.

First, cultivate the acquaintanceship of the people who live on either side of your rental property and across the street, exchanging telephone numbers with them. If they're like most neighbors, they'll be more than glad to call you if they see anything going on at your property that would likely upset you.

Second, make every effort to be there on the day the tenants move in. Check out whether they have any furniture of their own and how many people and animals actually intend to set up housekeeping there. You mustn't feel you're being nosy. This is YOUR PROPERTY they're taking over, and you want them to be at least vaguely aware of that.

A lot of people you rent to have a wholesome appearance but on moving day bring in some rather sleazy looking "relatives" you didn't know about. You may not be able to prevent this, ("My uncle is just staying here overnight!") but at least you can be aware of it and mentally prepare for the worst. (If you don't know the lingo, "worst" means "illegal goings-on".)

Third, when your friendly neighborhood informants let you know your tenants look like they're moving OUT, send your brother-in-law or some other man the tenants won't recognize to nonchalantly stand around and watch to see they don't accidentally take the doors, the bathtub, or the copper water pipes with them. He must be ready to call the cops at the drop of a hinge.

By now you must be wondering why I mentioned "slumlord or slumlady." Well, have you ever seen on television tenants complaining that their bad living conditions are the fault of a slumlord, as they point out to the TV cameras graffiti-covered walls, falling plaster, cracked toilets, and broken windows in their living quarters? Has anyone ever figured out who's causing these damages? Could it conceivably be the people who live there--the renters themselves?

A landlord should be the kind of person who finds it emotionally fulfilling to replace panes of glass, snake out drains, paint rooms, fill holes punched in walls, spray insecticide, haul away tons of trash--repairing, replacing and refurbishing a property in unending repetition.

98

A slumlord, on the other hand, may be a landlord who can't keep up with it any longer and surrenders, thinking that since the tenants keep destroying the property over and over, maybe that's the way they LIKE it.

So, learning all this and realizing that we weren't as smart as we'd thought we were, my husband and I got out of the landlord business as soon as we were able to find someone as unsuspecting as we had been to buy the place.

Then we lived in our single-family house with our seven children and spent the next several years trying to prevent THEM from destroying our property.

Anyway, now you know how you can become a slumlord or slumlady if you don't watch out.

Aunt Esther's Diet Tips

Before getting on a weight-loss kick, figure out whether you really ARE overly fat. (Don't guffaw--SOME people can't tell if they're fat just by looking in a mirror.) Get ahold of what's between your navel and your ribs. That's called the midriff bulge. If it's more than an inch thick, you're headed down Fat Street. Use a ruler if you like to kid yourself about such things.

Get on the scales and memorize the number that registers. (Of course don't tell anyone else what it is.) Look at one of those height/weight charts. Find the place that says "For Women Wearing 2-inch Heels" or "For Men Wearing 1-inch Heels." Put on shoes with the prescribed heel size and measure how tall you presently are. Then check out your ideal weight on the chart.

For each height, you get three sets of weights to choose among, depending on the size of your bones. You determine the size of your bones by comparing them with other people's. If you can't decide, choose Medium. Why not.

Then pick a desirable-weight number you like the sound of, and subtract it from the number you memorized on the scales. That's how many pounds you need to lose. WOW.

Next decide scientifically how active you are, without being a liar about it. If you run three or more miles four times a week, you're ACTIVE. If you walk around some, do a little housework, officework, or yardwork, you're SEMI-ACTIVE.

If you daily get out of bed, go to the bathroom, step in and out of the shower, eat a few meals and go back to bed, you're SEDEN-TARY, a really unpleasant word that reminds one of "sedimentary", a kind of rock layer that just lies there.

Next comes the hard part: trying to figure out mathematically how many calories you and your size bones need every day to lose weight, but not to get so HUNGRY you derange and begin to pack it in like a wild thing. If you don't know the math involved and don't even care to know it, just do it the easy way: simply eat around 1000-1500 calories a day. (In theory it's easy, anyway.)

Oh, by the way, if you're one of those ACTIVE persons I referred to, you're probably slim already and aren't even reading this.

Despite what you read in magazines, you can't possibly lose 15 pounds of fat a week even if you ingest nothing but black coffee and jump up and down all day. (Although you might find yourself blacking out now and then.) If you're really good at following a lower-cal plan, you might hit a pound-a-week average loss, and that's better than GAINING a pound a week.

Now for Aunt Esther's tips, suggestions and hints:

When you're at the food store, buy all the goodies in sight for your kids, spouse, roommate or favorite neighbors. So long as you're just planning on treating your loved ones, you know YOU won't eat any of it.

Remember that the bigger the size container you buy of a food, the cheaper it is per ounce. So if there's ever a truckload sale of M & M's or Peanut Butter Cups, for example, buy the whole load and save a great deal of money.

Speaking "Behavior Modification", never eat anywhere in the home except at the kitchen or dining room table. (Pick one.) This is to keep you from developing places all around the house that remind you to eat. If you ever find yourself eating candy bars and cashews in the bathroom and hiding the wrappers in dirty socks in the hamper, you'll recall this rule.

Don't grab a handful of food and eat dripping crumbs over the sink, but set out a pretty place mat, a tiny plate, a cup or glass, flatware and some frilly napkins. (The small plate is to dupe you into thinking your food looks bigger.) This all is supposed to make you feel satisfied after you eat a modest amount because you'll have enjoyed a high-class-type meal.

Actually, going to that bother cuts down on the time you have to spend on eating. You might even decide not to eat rather than fuss like that. (On the other hand, you might decide not to fuss like that but just eat. But YOU'RE the one who says you want to lose weight.)

Place a wastebasket nearby in which to drop the wrappers and any disposable containers. Then arrange the food in lovely colorful patterns on the plate. Don't read or watch television or play computer games while you eat. Concentrate only on consuming.

It takes about 20-25 minutes for your appetite to finally begin to feel satisfied, so if you want to get thin, don't pack in a lot quickly. One way to prolong the meal is to lay down your fork between bites of your ice cream, candy or nacho chips. Slowly count to one hundred before picking it up again.

As you'll notice when reading diet plans, there are certain groups of food you should choose from every day to keep healthy. The four famous groups are:

1)   Dairy: milk, cheese, butter, cottage cheese, yogurt.
2)   High Protein: meat, fish, fowl, nuts, eggs.
3)   Grain: rice, pasta, cereal, bread.
4)   Vegetables and fruit: vegetables, fruit.

So you NEED ice cream, bacon, cake, potato chips and cherry pie. They all fit in excellently with your body's nutritional requirements.

Keep your fridge stocked with lots of healthful fresh vegetables and fruits. Keep them in the covered storage bins, usually found at the bottom. After you've forgotten all about them for a time and they've become shriveled and/or moldy, discard them. Then go to the market and buy some beautiful fresh ones. Store them in the bins, etc.

When you're again at the store (see how many times a week you can fit food shopping into your schedule) always be on the lookout for new DIET FOODS.

There are sweeteners you can pour all over your food for a real no-cal taste treat. (The warnings on them about cancer are merely for laboratory animals.)

There are ice cream substitutes that look just like ice cream with chocolaty and fruity flavors, but have no cholesterol, no fat, no sugar, and a real strange flavor you may be able to endure.

There are entire diet-lite frozen dinners you can pick up, containing several OUNCES of food in lovely reusable containers, and they only cost three or four times what you'd spend if you went to all the aggravation of preparing them for yourself. (Although they're called "dinners", they do need a smattering of extras eaten along with them unless you're deliberately trying to famish.)

There are even diet cheesecakes, which are really delicious and can cut at least 12 calories out of your daily intake.

Now too you can get "spreads" having way fewer calories than regular butter or oleo. Although these diet spreads are one-half water, and you'll have to use twice as much to get any flavor on your bread or potatoes, you must try them. If it says "Diet" or "Lite", it's for you.

To be really careful to stay on your eternal diet, take rice cakes and low-cal salad dressing with you in your purse or briefcase to restaurants, parties and weddings, where there is a slight chance you might be tempted to overeat.

Dining at a restaurant poses special problems. First off, don't look at the menu; know ahead of time what you'll eat. Thus no wild temptations will cause your ruination.

Then order first, before your friends get the chance to order their high-fat plates which could move you to follow their lead in a monkey-see-monkey-do mode.

Get clear soup rather than creamed. Order your entree stripped of skin, bare of breading, boiled without oil, and naked of sauce. When you see the dessert tray come toward your table, run like hell out the door.

Eating at home might be simpler.

For gracious decorating at home, leave lovely crystal bowls of candy, pretzels and nuts around your living room. This will make both invited and drop-in guests feel you're a considerate host/hostess. Whether anyone visits or not, be sure to refill the bowls every time you notice them empty.

Another way to be considerate of others is to taste the food you prepare for them. Take a bite or sip after adding each shake of salt or sugar or oregano or garlic so that you don't accidentally sicken your loved ones.

If the food you're going to serve was pre-prepared, thoroughly taste it anyway before passing it around to make sure it's not stale or spoiled.

If you have small children somewhere in the family, stay with them on Halloween. You should know personally the people who give them goodies; if you're not absolutely positive something is safe for their delicate little insides, eat it yourself. Also eat all chocolate, nut and caramel treats so the little ones don't ruin their teeth. To be really safe, let them keep only the gum, pennies and apples.

The same thing goes for Easter. Protect them from the cruelty of biting off chocolate bunny heads by chewing up the bunnies yourself when the children aren't looking.

A good way to avert after-dinner all-evening television snacking is to brush your teeth right after your last food of the day. Be sure to have a large supply of toothbrushes and toothpaste on hand.

Drink 8 glasses of water daily besides your coffee, juice, pop and milk. This should help keep you away from the kitchen.

Only go food shopping immediately after having a heavy meal. Hopefully you won't buy much forbidden-type food if the mere sight of it makes you nauseated.

Try experimenting with the variety of weight-loss diets you'll find in women's magazines. These magazines all have incalculable numbers of diets and diet hints to help you. They also have innumerable recipes and full-color photographs of calorie-laden heaven-sent food for the time when you've finally lost all that extra weight and are ready to start gaining it back.

If you believe there are people who can make you lose weight even if YOU'RE not able to make yourself lose weight, join the club, the diet club that is. Logically, the more it costs to enroll, the better it should work. So if you can afford to spend a whole lot of money on NOT EATING, try any of a huge multiplicity of weight-loss groups.

If your friends can think of nothing to do for fun other than going out to eat, sit down with them soon and confer on finding other entertainments. If after a long talk session you come up with a list of recreational areas that have a real good restaurant in the vicinity, maybe you need new friends.

Now, if you follow Aunt Esther's diet tips but find that the number on the scales just keeps going up anyway, search out your local Overeaters Anonymous meeting and go to it. It's FREE, and they'll give you rules that actually make SENSE!

Stimulating Adult Education

These classes won't lead to a degree, or give you any kind of credits, or necessarily be adult, or even be especially educational, but the catalog says they will enhance and expand you, and they make a nifty piece of change for the teachers.

Here's a sizeable sample of courses to be found after sundown in many a neighborhood high school. Be sure to register as soon as the catalog hits your mailbox, because these classes fill up fast.

Accessorize With Swags

Decorating with handcrafted swags is the most exciting trend being seen today. Choose a swag that fits your style. The Christmas swag will be made of quality artificial greens and reds. The country swag will be made of dried flowers and paper-twist bows. The Victorian swag will be made with all the above plus lace, silk, and human hair. Your color choices will be mauve, puce, guava, and liver.

Archaeology for Beginners

How to retrieve by scientific methods such things as buildings, tools, pottery, graves, septic tanks, and gum relics found stuck under counters--all giving testimony of man's life and culture in former times.

Art Techniques for Beginners

Designed for the beginning artist to learn basic drawing skills. You will examine contour, negative space, portrait, perspective, and naked-women drawing. You will be using pen and ink, chalk and eraser, crayons and eyebrow pencils.

Astrology, Beginning

Learn the meanings of the signs, planets and houses as well as the math needed to invent your natal chart. Requirements are: knowing when you were born.

Astrology, Intermediate

Learn natal chart interpretation and how to include the influence of the transiting planets and the transiting space debris sent up into orbit by the U.S. and Russia.

Astrology, Continuing

For the semi-professional magician with advanced knowledge of astrology. Instruction will include a review of the fundamentals covered in previous Astrology classes, as well as an update on the changes taking place in the universe today such as the Spy in the Sky launched in 1990 and the utter proliferation of UFOs.

This course can be repeated as often as can be tolerated.

Basketweaving

Create a variety of functional country baskets that add a touch of warmth and clutter to any room in your home. In each four-week session you will complete six different baskets. These make perfect Christmas or Easter gifts for the people on your list who "hate everything."

Brass Wall Arrangement

Introducing a new idea for your home decorating! Envision the loveliness of a shiny plastic pot that fits flat against the wall, filled with Spanish moss, an assortment of dried flowers, popular pods, long slender leaves of eucalyptus, and other green leftovers you would otherwise put out with the trash, artfully arranged to measure 5 by 5 upon completion. Color options are pumpkin, radish, rutabaga and pumice.

Bridge

For anyone who in his spare time wants to build a bridge with cards. Basic bidding and bricklaying are covered.

Calligraphy (Hand Lettering)

A basic course for the beginner in the art of fancy lettering. Covers the proper use of materials and various techniques. Matting, mounting, illumination, darkening and charred edge antiquing will also be taught. You may well be the first human to discover what to gain or accomplish with this skill.

Candle Centerpiece

Nothing could be easier to make than this candle centerpiece! That's why we're charging a fee to teach it to you. Whether Christmas or good old Country, you'll learn how to decorate a single candle with either Christmas miscellany, or color-coordinated diced craft materials in country colors of frog green, sparrow tan, mushroom grey or porch swing pimiento.

Cartooning & Comic Book Art

Storytelling through the use of single or sequence illustrations. Caricature, character creation, composition and a superficial sense of humor will be among topics covered. Some familiarity with the pencil will be helpful but not essential.

Christmas French Horn

A symbol of noel, this 28" brass French horn, decorated with evergreens, baby's breath, butterfly's breath, mosquito's breath, traditional Christmas flowers, ribbons, bows, baubles, bangles and beads is a sure winner. If you have room somewhere to store it intact, it can be enjoyed every Christmas year after year.

Cut & Pierced Lampshades

Create charming candlestick lamps reminiscent of colonial times when there was little heat. A cut and pierced lampshade can add a touch of warmth to any room. You will learn how to deface a 4" X 6" scalloped shade, as well as how to add soft magic marker touches for an exceptionally exquisite effect.

Decorated Grapevine Wreath

Hang this artfully decorated grapevine wreath in your entry hall, dining room, or country kitchen for a look of natural beauty and a clout to the head of any tall man in your home. This wreath is garnished with your usual dried flowers, popular pods, fake greens, and a trendy paper bow with streamers that gently twist and turn for the finishing touch of entangling in the tall man's hair. Color options are black and blue.

Drawing for Beginners

This course will cover the basic abc's of drawing including composing, shading, perspective, color mixing and how to use a pail when drawing water.

Fiber-Covered Plaster

Friends will wonder how you ever made these unusual fiber-covered plaster cats, bunnies, ducks, sheep and tapirs. Learn how to adhere fabric to the plaster animal, smoothly brush on fifteen coats of glop, hand paint detailed physical features, and finish with a shiny glaze for a professional or sleepy look.

German, Conversational

Develop listening and speaking skills suitable for travel or casual conversation by learning basic words and idiotic idiomatic expressions. Class is guaranteed not to make you sound like Hitler or Mel Blanc.

Glass Blowing

Although modern methods have made glass blowing outmoded, it is still a hot hobby, raising the temperature in the workroom to sweltering proportions. We will be using melted-down spectacles, marred paperweights, broken drinking glasses, scrap mason jars and anything else you can obtain free of charge to blow into bizarre new art forms for your home.

Instant Papier-Mache Holiday Decorations

Crafting has never been so easy and so useless! Using newly developed products, you can create charming holiday decorations with no mess or time involved. Your choices are an old-fashioned "Mother Christmas" or a delightfully sweet chocolate-scented "Bunny". (To be kept away from children under age 3.)

Italian, Conversational

Have fun learning to speak the language of Michelangelo, Leonardo DaVinci, Perry Como, and many other great prodigies from the boot-shaped land of enchanting scenery, art, music, poetry, and pizza pies.

Painted Canvas Holiday Decorations

Enjoy making actual reproductions of imitation antiques. These painted pyramid-shaped canvas Santas for Christmas and bunnies for Easter can be proudly displayed right on your front porch! Routine holiday patterns will be transferred to the canvas, painted with paint, glued with glue, and shaped into a triangle. Santa has droopy ears attached.

Video Home Movie Making

A beginning course in the use of home cam-corders to make video home movies and really funny tapes to send to television programs. Topics covered will be how to use the controls and how to make documentaries. It is recommended you have a video camera in this class so that you have something to do with your hands.

Photography 35 MM Color

Covers the fundamentals of color photography with both slide and print films. Teaches what a camera is for, where the electronic flash is, what button to press, and what hole to look through. Also explains how to get the film in and out without demolishing it.

Stained Glass/Leaded and Copper Foiled

This class covers the basic skill of cutting glass into various sharp pieces. Leaded projects will be window hangers and candle holders (for those of you without electricity). Copper foil projects will be toilet tissue holders, parakeets in a hoop, and little baseless mirrors.

Tole Decorative Painting

Tole decorative painting is the method of painting designs on any object to decorate or to make a picture. No painting talent is necessary. After the object is spray painted, little Easter decals will be used. You just spit and stick.

Victorian Mirrors

Brighten a bare spot on your wall with this gorgeous mirror decorated in Victorian style. (No up-to-date craft person tolerates bare spots on his/her walls!) You will learn how to artfully decorate the outer edges of a round mirror with delicate baby's breath, microscopic silk flowers, and lacey strings. Color options are baby blue, kitten pink, puppy puce and kiwi green.

Wood Carving

A basic course for the beginner. Tools and techniques will be demonstrated and practiced. Three little useless wooden objects will be sculpted. Bring own carving knife.

Wood Turning

Basic course for the person who has always wanted to turn wood. Instructions will include proper procedures for mounting projects in the lathe and the safe use of the turn-on switch. Not recommended for students with weak fingernails. Enjoy the feeling of creativity and hypnosis as you watch the wood turn.

Guitar

Guitar for the beginner will cover how to strum, how to pick, how to make rhythm, how to play chords, and lastly how to make music. In tune with all the rest of our classes, you are taught country strumming. Therefore this class is not intended for the student who hopes to join a rock group.

Piano For Adults

Each class is three weeks long, and you can't take the second until you've taken the first. The third must be taken last. And although this might shock some eager learners, access to a piano to practice on outside of school is required.

Dancing, Ballroom (Couples)

For beginners, or a refresher course for those who have not been dancing for forty years. Instruction in many popular American, Indian and African dances along with tips on style, leading, and nose-piercing. Bring your own partner, as this is not a make-out class.

Dancing, Ballroom (Singles)

This course is designed for people without partners. You will dance with a classmate who doesn't know how to dance either. Meet new people, make new friends. This is a make-out class.

Dancing, Polka

Learn to do the Standard Polka, the Polish Hop, the Chairdash, the Pole Vault, and innumerable variations. A selection of Polka Line Dances will be included for you who like this sort of ethnicity.

Aerobics, Low Impact

A low energy program that gives you a meek cardiovascular workout intended for the delicate ones among you. Will not bounce, jounce, trounce or jar you. Some stretching, yawning, and unusual Lotus positions involved. Relaxation techniques also incorporated. Night gowns and pajamas recommended.

Aerobics, High Impact

A high energy program that gives you a prodigious workout. Certified Safety Instructors teach you to live it up and wear it out. You need your doctor's permission, and must wear high-test orthopedic safety shoes and muscle suits, including sturdy bras or sturdy jockstraps.

Aquarobics

Water exercise for fun and fitness. You don't have to know how to swim or even get your nose wet. All of the exercises will be done in the shallow end of the pool or on the surrounding floor. The more strenuous aspects are water jogging (like you do in a bad dream), and holding onto the edge and splashing like hell.

Fly Fishing

Have you ever wanted to experience fishing with flies? Learn the techniques of casting flies into water, how to test a stream for location of fish, how to catch the fish when they begin to eat the flies, and how to eat the fish when you tire of casting flies.

Golf--Chipping and Putting

Learn to chip and putt. Personalized videotape instruction with emphasis on chipping and putting. Bring own chipper and putter to class.

Karate For Self-Defense

Class is legally not allowed to teach Karate for offense, only for self-defense. A Korean-style program for you who like the idea of beating up others in defending the self. Men: sign up for this class as soon as possible because so many women enroll so quickly, there may not be room for you. Wear a belt-free white smock. Belts are not permitted unless they have been won in a class free-for-all.

Skiing, Cross-Country

Enjoy learning Nordic-type cross-country skiing. Actually it's speed-walking with short skis strapped to your feet. No downhill sliding is involved, except accidentally. A rental fee of $20 will cover skis, poles, boots and 40 pounds of warm clothing.

T'ai Chi Ch'uan

The first week is spent learning how to say and spell it. It is a form of meditational self-defense. Its gentle movement, flowing with our own bodies, reveals the body/mind/soul in harmony and lends power to the punch we mete out to our enemy's soft face and delicately centered nose. Promotes health, relaxation, skill and brazen recklessness.

Tennis

Includes instruction on the grip, swing, stance, backhand, forehand and midhand. Class also teaches the half volley, overhand volley, underhanded volley, and the drop kick. Bring racket and several cans of balls to class.

Volleyball, Co-Ed

Reviews volleyball skills plus participation in man-woman, boy-girl team play. This class is intended for those interested in inter-gender socializing and who already know how to play volleyball. This way we don't have to hire an instructor.

Yoga

Yoga is a natural easy way to revitalize the body through exercises that require comfortable everyday clothing, little strain and no effort. It involves nearly nothing.

Swimming, Beginners

This is for persons who have a REAL FEAR OF WATER. The pool is only filled one-foot deep. Basic principles are covered such as: floating, stroking, kicking and breathing. The crawl, back stroke, side stroke, and frantic stroke are also included.

Flower Arranging

Designed for beginners who wish to learn to work with fresh, silk, nylon, wool, cardboard, dried, and play-dough flowers. Basic flower arranging. Bring your own pot.

Gardening, Flowers & Vegetables

Teaches good gardening skills. For just dimes, you can have heaps of fresh flowers and vegetables to smell and eat. Learn sowing, soil prep, organic gardening, disease control, and how to terminate the bunnies and bambis that try to make a meal out of all your hard work.

Landscaping for the Home Owner

Learn how to give your outdoor property a professionally cared-for look. Proper planting, spacing, feeding, fertilizing, watering, mowing, spraying, pruning, and insect control will aid in beautifying your habitat and taking up hours and hours of your spare time.

Soil Improvement

This consists of making use of everything that comes out of your house in garbage bags or sewer pipes, and keeping it in one large contained heap as far out in the back yard as possible until it tries to crawl away by itself. Then you thoroughly mix it with your garden soil while wearing a gas mask. You'll have the best garden in the neighborhood.

Bonsai Tree Art

This course is designed for the beginning Bonsai enthusiast. Learn how to create and care for the trees you have stunted. These tiny trees take up very little space and give you an artistic outlet for the desire to maim something. Student must use highest priced concave pruners and bud shears, which can only be purchased through the instructor.

Introducing Antiques

Many lovers of garage sales, auctions, second-hand shops, attics and curb-side trash pickup day want to learn how to recognize an antique when they see one. Here's your opportunity! Course will focus on antique glass, pottery and old mattresses.

Bricklaying for the Handyman

Learn to build small brick projects at home, maybe some little outhouse-type thing for the back yard. Course designed for those who never before held a brick in their hand. Students get hands-on experience.

Electric Wiring

A course designed to assist the home owner with common electrical repairs and installations. Learn to do your own wiring and save all kinds of money! Class also touches on putting out fires between walls.

Small Appliance Repair

Save MORE money! Learn how to make electrical repairs on small appliances such as toasters, coffee pots, electric fry pans, lamps, and home computers. (TV and refrigerator repairs not included.) Includes tips on what to do in case of electrocution.

Repair, Refinishing

Actual reconditioning of furniture brought in. Remove old finishes, repair frames and blemishes, bleach, tone, and apply antiquing to impart that OLD look, like the finish you just removed. Bring only items that will fit through the classroom door.

Plumbing

Classroom and shop learning experiences designed to help the average guy or gal do the routine plumbing jobs they can't afford hiring a real plumber for. If you have a delicate stomach, you can purchase one of our professional gas masks for use in your real-life plumbing situations.

Sign Language for Everyone

A course open to all persons interested in learning the sign language of the deaf. Included is finger spelling and the use and comprehension of sign language. The course is all oral, so no deaf students, please.

Appetizers for Every Occasion

Serving a variety of appetizing appetizers is a great way for family and friends to gather together for renewing friendships and breaking diets. In this demonstration class, you will learn how to prepare potato lumps with sour cream, sausage puffs, eel fritters, and a blueberry and liver pate.

Cake Decorating

Basic skills for all-occasion cakes. Level 1 includes simple borders, figure piping, transferring photos, and buttercream flowers. Level 2 will teach edelweiss flower creation, wafer painting, and snowflake impressions, all done on a cardboard circle that can be duplicated at home on an actual cake.

Healthy Eating With Whole Grains

For today's health fanatic, this course will focus on cooking with whole grains and learning their nutritional values. Class will assemble in the field next door to get first-hand knowledge of picturesque and wholesome grains, with possibly some delicious mushrooms thrown in.

Christmas Gingerbread Church

From your own oven comes a most enchanting Christmas spectacle! You will learn how to make a frosted gingerbread church and steeple surrounded by decorated Christmas trees, carolers, ice skaters on a pond, and a horse pulling a sleigh with bells on. Can be illuminated if desired with a 3-foot string of edible Christmas tree lights.

Introduction to the Wok

Get acquainted with your wok! In this demo class you will learn how to use a wok for preparing traditional Moo Goo Pie Pan made of chicken, bok choy, water chestnuts, mushrooms and cherries in a flavorful sauce of butterscotch and crushed Brazil nuts. Also the ever-popular pepper steak made of bison tenderloin strips simmered with green peppers, onions, and seedless figs.

Microwave Cooking

It's time to start using your microwave for more than heating and reheating! Learn the latest cooking techniques, major features and benefits of microwaves. Through lecture and hands-on experience you will prepare lovely homemade pretzel fluffs and petrified bacon chips. Before your eyes cakes will rise and corn will pop, butter will explode and boiling water will overflow its container. Lab fee covers microwave cleanup.

Reading Food Labels for Better Health

Are you a victim of "decision" burnout? The average shopper is dazed with 190,000 food products every time he steps into the supermarket. In this class you'll learn the parts of a food label, the significance of those little black lines, and the real meaning of terms such as lite, lo-cal, no-cal, low-salt, low-sodium, slo-mo, etc. Bring food labels from those foods you eat and we'll try to decipher them.

Tofu

Learn how to use this all-purpose soy food that is high in protein and calcium, low in calories and sodium, and 100% yogurt free. You will make and eat a terrific pizza that will fool many a meat eater, be it cat or dog, and a spinach tofu combo that can be served over ice cream. You will make tofu-burgers, tofu-furters, and a cheese-like filling to stuff pasta shells or pillow covers, and much more. Tofu can be found somewhere in your local grocery store.

Counted Cross Stitch

Counted cross stitch is a simple-minded needlework hobby that only looks difficult because of the delicate color shading that can be achieved using 75 different shades of thread. Learn the basics for an inexpensive hobby. You will complete a looped picture of a simple country house with a tiny country heart at the top of the smoking country chimney. Cigarets not included.

Updating Old Clothes

Fabulous new techniques and products have made clothes-decorating a wonderful new hobby for all ages and sexes. Rubber stamp printing, silk screening, stenciling, acrylic painting, fabric markers, and painted elbow macaronis are some of the ways you can update and rejuvenate your old clothes.

Quilting

Create a legacy; a quilt beautifully designed and stitched with love and adoration will become a treasured heirloom for the ones who come after you. Included in this class will be hand quilting, foot quilting, applying applique, and hemming and hawing the edges.

Rug Hooking

Who among us has not one day wanted to make their own rug? Learn this art which originated with the early settlers, who had nothing else to do in the winter but try to keep warm. Designs can be colonial, oriental, or French Canadian to suit your decor. Using a special hook similar to a tiny crochet hook but the size of a Captain Hook hook, you'll learn how to create a swarm of loops which quickly become a rug under your incessant hooking. Yes, who among us has not one day wanted to be a hooker.

Sewing - I and II

The sewing I class is designed for the person who has no sewing experience and would like to learn how to thread a needle and make a knot that won't come undone. Many of today's fashions have simple lines that can be made with just those sewing skills. Sewing II continues on to teach you how to thread a needle and get knots that won't come undone using a sewing machine.

Accessorizing with Scarfs

Accessorizing with beautifully colored scarfs will expand your wardrobe and update it for today's fashionable look. (Yesterday's look was unfashionable.) Hundreds of techniques for tying scarves on various parts of the body will be taught.

Accessorizing with Scarfs and Clips

Update your wardrobe once more, with scarfs and scarf clips. You may never again need to buy new clothes if you take our courses. Using a 3-foot square scarf and a single faux gold scarf clip, we'll teach you how to create an utter surfeit of fashionable styles!

Business Etiquette

Learn how to develop a sense of ease for social and business events. Being able to perform comfortably and confidently while someone is looking will make others imagine you are an assured, confident person and will establish an impressive, if false, image in their minds. Learn to greet strangers, make introductions, make small talk easily (with special emphasis on weather terms), and feel composed even if you get a broken fingernail, a run in your hose, or your underpants fall down around your ankles.

Body Language

When you meet someone for the first time, you are evaluated within the first two seconds by how you look and speak. That impression can be irreversible! You will learn strategies to improve your chance for success by using the correct body language so the other person knows exactly what you mean without your telling him. Topics covered will be the one-eyebrow lift, the scowl, the sneer, the nose-pinch, the near-miss karate chop, and the finger pointing into the mouth designating the desire to vomit.

Hair Styling and Image Makeover

This course is designed for the active woman who would like to improve her appearance without having to sit still very long. Instruction will include setting, styling, coloring, blow drying, crimping, primping, permanent waving, and cutting one's own hair using only two hands and one mirror. You will also learn how to wash your face, brush your teeth and cut your own fingernails and toenails. This class is for your own personal use and does not entitle you to be a real beautician.

Receptionist Training

Receptionists unknowingly represent their employers to the public. Class will teach you how to dial a telephone, how to say "Hello, please sit down" to visitors (greet 'n seat), how to write suitable messages on a message pad, how to walk when you tell someone to "walk this way", and how to make and serve coffee without spilling it on the phone. Taking a typing class while getting Receptionist Training would increase a participant's career opportunities.

Administration of Medications

This course is designed for the nurse who needs to update his/her medical skills. Teaches you how to induce the patient to open his mouth without biting your fingers; to swallow a pill and not hide it under his tongue; and to not ingest any medicine that spilled on the floor or pill that got dropped into the toilet unless first okayed by the doctor.

If these subjects haven't piqued your interest, the schools will be coming out with updated catalogs of even more exciting courses and classes next spring. Be watching for them in the mail!

MAN Magazine
(How to be a Man in What's Fast Becoming a Woman's World)

The overriding theme in MAN Magazine is:

Let's get dressed up, made up, slimmed down, ear-pierced, concoct irresistible meals, and create a beautiful home, all in the hope of getting our constant concern and main goal in life--a woman.

Here are examples and samples of what you will discover in upcoming articles:

Food

Making Gorgeous Desserts

Preferably you don't present Sarah Lou frozen compounds to your Woman, but instead spend a lot of money on things like goat cream, out-of-season gooseberries, exotic liqueurs, imported high-smelling cheeses, non-toxic mushrooms, foreign nuts and such.

How to Set a Lovely Table

Don't use plastic forks or napkins snitched from a fast food restaurant. Mismatched silverware is also prohibited. Be prepared to at least set a table for TWO that has matched flatware and un-chipped dishes. Use a tablecloth. If you've never owned one, go out and buy one. Women prefer white ones with lacy edges. (Cloth, not paper, please.)

If you really want to impress Her, use a centerpiece. That means a lovely bowl of fragrant flowers and two candle holders bearing short fat candles (ones that won't tip over and burn the new tablecloth.)

Fashion

Beachwear

We will feature captivating photographic layouts of bathing apparel that uncovers almost the whole shebang, if you've got the shebang for it. We also show fetching bathing apparel that COVERS a lot, if that's your bag.

Fashion Makeover

This monthly feature shows how one of today's men looks in all the wrong dowdy clothes, and then how he looks in all the right MOD clothes. We feature a different gentleman every month. Readers can enter into the fun by sending in a photograph of themselves showing how badly they dress.

The New Male Jewelry

Single earrings, or the new daring double earrings (two in each ear!), zircon-encrusted tie bars, and the innovative jeweled BEARD accessories. The modern male is not afraid to wear jewelry to attract women. He knows it makes women think he's extremely self-confident or rich.

Styles for the Large Man

Luckily, men are never obese, but just large, strong or macho. Now that the fashion world admits not ALL men are a size 34, we reveal the latest styles that help flatter and flatten the HE-MAN. "Just His Hugeness" brand underwear and rubberized cummerbunds are stressed.

Finding the Right Jock Strap

Now stores have someone to HELP you find the right fit, unlike the olden days when you could only find "one size fits all".

Personal Handsomeness

Hair Makeovers

Photo essay on how he looked in his old high school hair style, and how he looks now in his new up-to-the-minute hairdo. We present three of these in every other issue. Readers can enter into this makeover too, by submitting a photograph of themselves and their current outdated hairdo.

How to Clean the Hair

Nowadays men don't merely knead a hunk of soap into their hair and think it does the job. That causes dandruff, grease buildup, and scum! Today's man wants beautiful hair to woo the woman of his dreams. That means shampoo, dandruff dip, conditioner, grease-blast, moisturizer, color enhancer, blow-dry gel and mousse. (Until the cosmetics industry can come up with additional indispensable steps in hair care.)

Hair Color

The older gentleman at the top of the corporate ladder knows how important artificial youth is. He colors his hair and is proud of it! Every edition of MAN Magazine brings exciting new shades and forms of hair colorization: froth, foam, gel, slather, slither, and spritz-on. Don't miss a single issue!

Makeup

Even more exciting than fashion makeovers or hair makeovers are our make-out MAKEUP makeovers. We'll show you how to acquire a glowing blush-like complexion, passionate King-Kong eyebrows, luscious lips, bedroom eyes. A great new fashion fad is chromeplating the toenails so that She'll sit up and take notice!

To enter into the fun, send a photo of your face bare of all makeup but with whatever hair covering you currently cultivate, and you may be one of the lucky fellows to be featured in a future makeup makeover!

Fragrances

A real man, of course, doesn't wear perfume. However, even before he steps out the door in the morning, he does put on a touch of FRAGRANCE. Modern men are no longer sissies about doing something they really desire to do and see a need for, and so they buy and use just gallons of the luscious new male scents.

Have you ever seen a real woman pass by a new leather jacket, open spice jar, bag of just-ground coffee, or fresh flowers and not lean over, sensually put her face into them, and inhale deeply? Well, then?

Health

Shapeup

We present the ever-desired exercises, ones which make large things smaller (waistlines, hips), and yet also make small things larger (muscles). Fortunately for us, women prefer men with muscles on the "normal" side. Huge bulging muscles delight their eyes but may frighten them away from the man who lugs them around. Sorry, Tarzan.

Diets

We'll feature diets designed to help you lose weight, banish cellulite, live to be 90, rev up your sex life, increase head hair growth, prevent broken fingernails, and lengthen the eyelashes.

Sex

The Other Man

Hints and tips on what to do to get Her back into your bed. Also hints and tips on what to do if you don't WANT her back, including such important data as how to change the locks on your doors and how to find a cost-efficient lawyer.

What to do If She Loses Interest in Sex

Same as above.

What to do If You Lose Interest in Sex

It can never happen.

Your Horoscope

Each issue lets you look to the stars to discover what sign to search for (other than Beware of the Dog or Keep Out) when you're seeking a mate. To learn what times of the month are the best for finding love-without-viruses. To seek an answer to the chilling questions, "What should I say to the waiter in case my woman forgets her credit card and I forget my wallet?" or "She seems to love me, but will she love my parakeet?"

ASK ALBERTO

Our very own Guru, Alberto, can tell you what to do when your monthly horoscope doesn't have the answers you seek. This should be most of the time. Send your questions to "ASK ALBERTO" at the address on the masthead of the magazine. You can have complete faith in his advice because he holds degrees in the fields of psychiatry, social counseling, law, tailoring, and tele-theology.

Home Care and Crafts

Upcoming issues will show you:

- How to knit a romantic sweater to surprise her on her birthday.
- How to crochet an afghan-for-two for those dreamy evenings spent on the chilly couch.
- Using simple materials found around your house, how to devise slipcovers to hide seedy furniture.
- How to raise, care for, slaughter and cook a turkey for her Thanksgiving.
- How to utilize small spaces so that she'll find your home warm and comfortable, not stark and empty. (Statistics show that women have an inborn desire to see all spaces in an abode filled.)

Plants

Develop a green thumb, because no windowsill or any other spot where a smatter of sunlight falls should be barren of plants in pots. This reiterates the statistics above.

Manly Collections

Examples of some collections to give you enjoyment and to impress Her: Miniature guns (real guns might frighten a feminine person), oriental unicorns, chess sets made from shark teeth, war figurines, male dolls. Male dolls are ones with a penis. These dolls are extremely rare but interesting.

Meeting Women

How to Meet Ms. Right

- Walk a cute dog.
- Visit flea markets (without the dog), garage sales, and all craft shows in your vicinity.
- Take evening classes in quilting and cake decorating.
- Join a church where they allow female clergypersons.
- Make friends with your neighborhood gynecologist.

These and many other items of earnest interest to men will be highlighted in future issues of MAN Magazine. You'll find MAN a sure winner!

MAN'S Motto: I'm a male, a man, and I'm a-worth it!

How to Avoid Being Taken In
(Deceived, Duped, or Tricked)

Lately I have the strange sensation that everywhere I go there's Something/Someone urging me to BUY something.

It displays beauty before my eyes, sings music into my ears, wafts lovely smells into my nose from the pages of scratch-n-sniff, and urges samples into my mouth in the aisles of the supermarket.

Its strongest appeal is visual, emanating at me from my TV set and from every newspaper and magazine in sight. It makes me feel sexy, safe, cozy, down-homey, wise, beautiful, smug, intelligent, back in the good old days, and rich.

In the midst of enchanting sensual input, a banal object appears. In my mesmerized mind, I begin to connect the inane object with the delightful feelings. I almost go right out and BUY the boxed pie, the eyelash stretcher or the house slippers in the hope of capturing those feelings.

Something/Someone

I picture this as an ever-burgeoning group of nameless, faceless people who spend eight hours a day sitting around conference tables thinking up ways to induce us to hand over our earnings.

To save ourselves from big-time waste of money, let's look closer at the things we're being prodded to buy, and ponder some pointed questions, namely:

Why would I (or anyone) want to buy the object in question?

That is, what's the purpose of it? What can it be used for? What GOOD will I get out of it?

If I buy the object, will I attain the lovely feelings aroused by the advertisement? For how long? Are the feelings worth putting out the dough for?

Think of the dough. Are there other, more desirable ways I'd rather spend that money? If I save up the money I might've spent on many little inanities, will I someday be able to buy something big with it, like maybe a cruise?

If it's something I really need, won't I be just as happy if I buy a cheaper one than the one the ads are prodding me to get?

Some of The Advertised Things

Perfume

Perfume, or re-named for men "fragrance", is an expensive smell you put on for an unknown purpose. Perfume started out as a means to camouflage vile body odors in the days when people hardly ever bathed. Advertising has yet to explain why you should wear perfume now.

Maybe it's supposed to thrill you to hear someone say "I like your perfume. What's the name of it?" This actually may happen to you. (Oddly, it happened to me recently. I didn't quite know what to say, since I wasn't wearing any.)

How thrilled would you be if you could hear what people around you may be THINKING: "Her perfume stinks. She must've taken a bath in it! Give me AIR. Pee-yoo!" I've often had these musings, especially when confined with a perfumee in an office, bus or elevator.

Irritably speaking, who besides a dog goes around trying to smell other people anyway? Isn't being clean good enough?

The ads insinuate that we buy perfume to wear to social events with the goal of arousing someone's sexual interest. If that's the purpose, why do married women and men wear fragrances to work? Hmm?

If a perfume has the name of a Famous Person, people presumably buy it to be in some mystical way LIKE that person. Since the fragrance won't make those who use it rich, famous, or beautiful, it must make them naive.

If a company calls their perfume "Ugly" and you put some on, will you turn ugly?

Soap

It's nice to wash oneself. Washing removes dirt, dead skin, germs, grease and bad smells. A bar of cheap soap does the trick.

But Something/Someone wants us to spend MORE. So it invented liquid soap, soapless soap (cold cream), and soap for dry skin (which doesn't remove oil as well as regular soap), then added lovely colors and multiple perfumes to wrest extra money from us and provoke strange allergies.

Some products come right out and say they are allergy-free. Supposedly this means you can't get a rash, wheeze or itch from them. But despite any such claim, EVERYTHING CAN CAUSE AN ALLERGY IN SOMEONE SOMETIME. (Sounds like a song title).

Moisturizers

It was noticed that soap removes oil from our skin. So we must replenish it with moisturizer. This was a chance to make all degrees of grease-ADDING mixtures and talk us into thinking we need them.

Dry lips were brooded over. Petroleum jelly works but it's much too commonplace and inexpensive. Lip balms in a stick were invented, tiny supplies of a waxy substance at an incredible price per pound.

Someone might see our hands, so they came in for special attention. They do get awfully chapped, especially in wintertime. Good old petroleum jelly again, right? Look on the shelves and be stunned by the number of "hand therapy" products you find there, each having the same lone effect: keeping your natural water from leaving your skin through its outer layer.

There are oils to float on your bathwater or smear your entire body with after bathing, which seems yucky but might appeal to some. The labels omit mentioning that human skin normally oils itself up for free.

Hair Products

Like soap, shampoo takes out grease and dirt. Conditioner adds a little gunk so the hair doesn't stand straight up when it dries. Mousse and hair spray add a glue-like stiffener that helps your hair stay in whatever strange shape you put it in. O.K.

But hot-oil hair treatment? First you totally saturate your hair with oil. Then before you can GO anywhere, you must completely wash the oil out. That's it. I don't get it.

Laxatives, Nasal Sprays

Nostrums that do exactly what they say they'll do. But when you stop using them, the original problem tries to come back worse than it was at the start. Generating an addicted following is a real handy way to make money. It reminds you of the tobacco industry, doesn't it.

Toothpaste

There are presently 3 kinds of toothpaste: tartar control, breath freshener, and regular. If you need a tartar controller to clean your teeth, and a breath freshener to make your breath smell good, what do you need the regular for? On the other hand, if the regular toothpaste cleans teeth and freshens breath, why the two other kinds? (There are also a couple brands that must be made with a concentrate of red-hot peppers, because they burn your mouth so strongly. Does this supposedly cremate the germs at the same time?)

Liquid Diet Meals

Tasty but monotonous meals that can in fact help people to lose weight. When these people stop drinking the stuff and go back to eating food, they gain the weight back. This is called the Eater's Law of Inevitability.

Women's Personal Bathroom Products

Mothers and daughters smiling smugly and hinting about products that mysteriously make you feel confident. Young women telling each other the "news" about something so absorbent you can hide a quart in it. Older women glad they can now get out into the world again--same type of product but different problem. Another woman delighted because she now knows whether she's pregnant or not and it's only been six hours!

To be equitable, men too should do ads like these. Two guys, ten years apart in age, pretending to be father and son chatting about intimate products. Young fellows sitting around in front of mirrors, combing their hair and talking about using shorts liners or masculine hygiene spray to feel fresh. Or a husband glowing with joy because now he'll know whether his wife is pregnant even before the obstetrician does.

Animal Food

Fancy-shaped dog food. Oh, PLEASE. Your dog couldn't care less if his food has cute little shapes, a variety of colors, or an interesting selection of flavors. He's color-blind, shape-blind, and will eat week-old turkey bones from a stranger's garbage can if you don't stop him.

Didn't you ever watch your dog eat? If the smell suits him at the moment, he wolfs it down in several gulps and away he goes. Do you actually think he NOTICED the colors, the shapes, or even the flavors? Does he feel well loved because his owner is ditzy?

The same thing goes for your CAT and her food too.

And those bone-shaped dog cookies that are supposed to clean his teeth--doesn't he scarf them down just as fast as he does his regular, more cost-efficient food? Do you think you're cleaning your teeth if YOU eat real hard cookies?

Inane Objects

During every Christmas season, storekeepers bring out a great supply of odd objects to be sold for presents, then put away what's left over until the next year's Christmas frenzy.

These articles often look real handy: a complicated food processor that does everything to vegetables except eat them; a mechanical card shuffler that does four decks at a time (for those rare games that use four decks mixed together); a compass for the car (so you can find where you're going without having to wear your glasses); a Christmas-dessert cookbook featuring thirty ways to make pumpkin pie; tiny variously-shaped "crystal" containers too small to contain anything; a combo of cheap tools for personal hygiene comprising scissors, clippers, cuticle pushers and earwax spoons.

They're things you know YOU'D never use but somehow you think the persons on your Christmas list would. Don't look now, but after Christmas the recipients of these types of gifts will straightaway stow them in the attic or basement where they'll remain gathering mildew until the next of kin disposes of them.

Necessities

There are wonderful doohickeys that we all want and need and love to own, namely: a watch, a TV set, a car, clothes, a house. These can all be bought at reasonable prices. But Something/

Someone sits around the conference table and concocts SNOB APPEAL to spuriously raise prices and give us purchase urges.

Snob appeal tells us *"When Other People see you have THIS, they'll think you're more wonderful than they are!"* Notice it's not saying that the high-priced item is any better than the low-priced, only that owning it will impress other people with your greatness.

Here are some snob-appeal questions to ponder:

Does a watch smothered in diamonds tell time more efficiently than a discount-house special?

Does a wall-size TV set display more wonderful shows than a regular TV?

Does a fur coat made of sable keep you any warmer than a fur coat made of acrylic?

Does a house with seven bathrooms do anything more for you than a house with 1½? Would you really have a use for three ovens in your kitchen, or a closet you can take a hike in?

When you see an obscenely expensive car whish by, do you look in admiration at the person behind the wheel? Or do you think "Show-off!" Can those house-priced cars fly or something?

Do people really think highly of the billionaire? For instance, do you really like Donald Trump?

Examples of Snob Appeal

"Collection"

THE snob appeal word, utterly meaningless, used on everything from diamonds to cheap but expensive dime-store gloves. It doesn't mean your hobby, as in "my stamp collection."

Whenever you come across the word COLLECTION in an advertisement, know that Something/Someone wants you to pay more for the product than if it were just your ordinary object not ensconced in an imaginary collection.

Famous Name Brand

"These jeans aren't made in a building by actual people sewing up blue material and zippers like CHEAP jeans are. Hoochy-Koochy makes these jeans! They're magically created in a much more exceptional way than those no-name things!"

Jot this down on your shopping list: "Famous name brands cost more, not because they're necessarily BETTER than lesser-known or generic brands, but because they're ADVERTISED more." Always buy name brands if you enjoy the fun of helping large companies pay their overblown advertising bills.

Famous Person

Mr. or Ms. Famous uses and loves this product. How impressive. Either Mr. or Ms. Famous are far above you in some way and you should follow their lead, or they're being PAID to push the product. We all know what's going on here, don't we?

Bragging About The High Price

"Only rich people can buy THIS! Nyah nyah!" That may be true, but it doesn't follow that the article is any better than more sanely priced ones.

Terrible Problems

Nextly, Something/Someone spends a lot of time blowing up minor problems out of all proportion, and inventing imaginary ones to worry you about. Then they can formulate and noisily promote a PRODUCT for those dreadful problems. Namely:

Icky spots on glasses. Innumerable people have dishwashers and never heard of glasses developing repulsive spots until they learned of it in a commercial. The glasses shown in one ad look like someone sneezed a big one all over them.

Collar dirt rings. There are such things, but who really cares. When you launder, put extra detergent on the ring, same as on wrist or ankle rings. Have the family wash their necks better.

Big wet underarm circles. Wash underarms, dry underarms, apply a deodorant. Then keep your arms down and don't stick your armpits in anyone's face.

Dandruff. Surprise, surprise--EVERYONE has dandruff, so don't feel ashamed thinking you're the only flake in the crowd. If despite cleansing your scalp you still have fallout, shun black and try wearing colors and patterns that obscure little white flecks.

Bad breath. An innate human attribute. To diminish it, brush your teeth with toothpaste. Visit your dentist and doctor once in a while so there won't be anything reeking inside you that toothpaste and peppermint can't handle.

Flat hair. Gee, isn't that heartbreaking. Shampooing and combing it once in a while should fluff it up.

Split ends. Some people have hairs sporting double ends, like an eensie V. This fact is supposed to be bad, something you should buy products for, even though it's entirely meaningless to anyone's beauty or health. If split ends ever set you to worrying, get a haircut--instant cure.

Colors mysteriously disappearing from favorite clothes. I've never seen that happen, even with clothes like bright red T-shirts and new bluejeans that vividly bleed their dyes into the water when you wash them. By the time most clothes are discernibly faded, they're also ready for the rag bag.

Quack Products

These are not designed for your duck. These are designed to prey on your fears and arouse your wishful thinking. They hint at, or come right out and promise, cures for:

Small Bosoms

Nothing will enlarge them except a surgeon implanting bags of smush, or your gaining weight. Get fatter and your bust will grow. So will all the rest of you, especially your middle and bottom.

Pimples, Age Spots

If the remedies sold over the counter in drugstores worked, don't you think you wouldn't see so many people WITH these skin problems?

Red Veins in the Whites of Your Eyes

If you have a bad case of this, get to your eye doctor. If you have the little red veins that we all have and for some obscure reason think they mar your beauty, go straight to the drugstore, pick up

147

a bottle of red-removing eyedrops, and read the label. First it says it will TEMPORARILY remove the red. Next it says that if you use the product too many times in one day, your eyes will become MORE red. For this they want us to spend money?

Facial Aging

Makeup is supposed to hide wrinkles and droops. In real life, it accentuates them. As to the magic-formula skin creams that are supposed to make older skin appear young again, try this: buy the smallest size jar you can find and use it only on one side of your face for as long as the jar lasts. Then see if that side of your face has become younger or prettier; or if you've simply developed pimples on that side because of the cream's possible pore-plugging penchant.

If there's something about your body that you dislike, don't rely on Something/Someone. Ask a doctor for help. (And pray that the DOCTOR isn't a quack.) If medical science can't cure or improve your personal appearance problems, maybe you can find something else to fret about.

Contrived Holidays

Something/Someone also loves to invent new holidays. Then more people have to be placated, more guilt has to be felt, and more things have to be bought. Yes, right now you can hear off in the distance that old theme song, "BUY, BUY, BUY!"

Mother's Day

Little kids enjoy Mother's Day because it gives them a chance to make a present in school, like they enjoy making hand-silhouette turkeys for Thanksgiving, cardboard Easter baskets, Halloween jack-o-lanterns and whatever else the teacher can think up to keep the little tykes busy.

But do moms want all their grown kids to gather around on Mother's Day and gift Mommy with boughten things? Probably not. She's apt to feel bad that her kids spent the money, and she may not know what to DO with more things. (All except candy, of course. She'll know what to do with that.)

Most mothers only want a smile, a hug, and friendship from the kids; and they should give her those things all year around. That's my opinion, anyway. But talk against Mother's Day at the risk of your life!

The biggest trouble with Mother's Day is that THEN they had an excuse to go and invent Father's Day and Grandparent's Day. Grandchildren's Day, Aunt's Day, Uncle's Day, Niece's Day and Nephew's Day must be just around the corner.

Sweetest Day

Buy stuff, mainly candy, for everyone you care about. You'll notice that people who sell feminine type items such as jewelry and negligees push those things on Sweetest Day, like maybe men don't deserve sweetness. Other than spending more bucks uselessly, what's the basic meaning of Sweetest Day? (It's not true that a dentist invented it.)

149

Secretary's Day, Boss's Day, Office Cleaner's Day?

There are getting to be Special Days for every person, every occasion, every cause. That would be O.K. if you could ignore the Day (and some resolute people do), but you still may find yourself in for some squirming. For instance, your secretary may wonder *"What the hell?"* when she finds out the other secretaries in the building got presents on Secretary's Day but she didn't.

The big falsehood in all this is that we are morally obligated to BUY THINGS for people to show our appreciation or love or admiration. Who SAYS so? . . . Oh yes, Something/Someone.

Sneaky Advertising

Lastly, Something/Someone is inventing ways to advertise that don't SEEM to be advertising so they can smuggle their Buy Message into our subconscious. Then we won't say to ourself, "Hey, that's an advertisement--watch out!"

Movies inadvertently show specific products with their names prominently displayed. Newspapers and magazines have large spreads that look like exciting news except "Advertisement" is barely in sight somewhere on the page.

Something/Someone even now is planning to display wares to us in ways we haven't known before to take us by surprise and not leave us with a moment's free time to think our own thoughts.

It intends to fashion BUY BUY videotapes and play them:

By the gasoline pump, so you can be brainwashed as you pump your gas.

Inside your grocery cart and flashing you from each shelf in the supermarket, so you'll be unable to leave the store with any money at all left in your wallet.

On the oxygen tank facing you in the Recovery Room when you're coming out of anesthetic and are in a weird mental state.

Worst of all, our last haven may be breached. I hear they're trying to devise a way to get ads into our bathroom to amuse us on our Sit Break. I HATE to think what they'll come up with next!

So remember: uncaring of your real needs or your money situation, Something/Someone wants you to BUY. So wake up and smell the coffee--the generic kind.

How to be Safe Rather Than Sorry or Dead

Walking at Night

• Plan the route you'll take. Go only where it's well lit, many people are about, and you have a strong friend with you. If by following this rule you can't get to where you want to go, either travel in a locked vehicle or stay home.

• Dress discreetly. Don't dress provocatively (half naked) and have people mistake you for a prostitute. Also don't wear black if you expect drivers to be polite and not run over you.

• Don't leave your house or apartment key in a stupid hiding place. You know what I mean--under a door mat, hanging on a nail inside a screen door, on a rear window sill, or in a windowbox of flowers where the neighbor's cat can scrape at it, deposit on it, and then bury it.

• Get a sturdy totebag to carry with you, and put into it:
a flashlight,
a loud whistle or a gas-powered eardrum blaster,
emergency phone numbers (preferably also inked onto your skin somewhere in case your totebag is snatched),
a blunt or sharp instrument of crime prevention,
or a firearm. Many of us would love to carry a gun (pack a rod), but haven't figured out a surefire technique to get it out of the totebag, cock it, aim it, and shoot it before an attacker has a chance to snatch it out of our hand and shoot US with it.

We also don't relish the possibility of being jailed for carrying a concealed weapon. Or having our gun plop out of our purse or totebag and project its bullet into a harmless bystander or our own foot.

• Don't carry valuables with you. Leave them at home for the burglars to find.

• Stay out of and away from: back yards, dark deserted parks, alleys, underground parking garages, and condemned buildings.

• Watch for any guy who appears to be just standing around, loitering. Don't be embarrassed to start running the other way, even if you later realize he was probably just waiting for a bus.

• Shrieking loudly while you run can be beneficial, if you have the breath capacity for such a feat.

• If someone chases you, don't run home, because then he'll know where you live. Run somewhere else, preferably to a police station. In fact, all your after-dark traveling should be done in the vicinity of police stations.

Driving, Night or Day

• Don't drive with an empty gas tank.

• Always buy a car with air conditioning. That way you can drive around with your doors locked and your windows shut even in hot weather, safe from everyone but a nut with a brick.

• When parking, don't leave anything in the car that you couldn't live without lest the object gets stolen from the car or the car itself is gone when you get back.

• If you MUST lug things around, such as packages, put them in your trunk before you get to where you're going to park. Don't park first and then hide your stuff in the trunk while any nearby crook watches. Again, preferably do your parking by a police station.

• Before entering a car, check the back seat to see if someone is hunkered down there. (Remember all those scary movies?)

153

- Make sure your horn works. If it's one of those little tooters instead of a real beeper, get a louder one installed. Beep short blasts over and over if someone tries something. Hopefully that will scare him off rather than enrage him.
- If you suspect you're being followed by a creep in some other vehicle, drive to a police or fire or gas station and tell them you're being followed. If you can get them to believe you, they may offer to help.

   Or if you can find people walking along, pull over by them and watch the following car (hopefully) pass you by and drive on. Then YOU drive on to get away from the people, who may be eyeing you speculatively.
- If someone up to no good follows you into your driveway, stay in your locked car and BEEP. That's smarter than jumping out and trying to beat your follower in a foot race to your locked front door.

Using Public Transportation

- Sit near the driver, but not where someone can grab whatever you carry and leap out the door with it before you can even say "Hey, that's MINE!"
- Take a taxi to scary places (why are you going to scary places?) and have the cab driver walk you in. Presumably HE won't try to assault you.
- Don't leave your purse or briefcase sitting unattended in a grocery cart. Or on the floor in a restaurant, or in an empty seat at a movie. Or on the top of your car just before you drive away.
- Don't flash a wad. You shouldn't be carrying a wad, anyway-- it should be in the bank. We're talking money here, not chewing gum.

154

• Don't trust other women either in secluded places. There actually are female criminals.

• If you're a woman, don't wear high heels. Wear sneakers. Recall those scary movies where the woman always trips on her high heels and falls down at the most inopportune time.

* * * * * *

The main idea here is that wherever you go, there may be warped people who will try to harm anyone they find in an unwatched or unprotected setting. If nobody's around, they're gonna try to getcha!

So don't get paranoid--just get smart: completely trust no one but your closest family, dearest friends, and some of those people with the guns who are manning and womaning our police stations.

Hints on Tips

Magazines, newspapers and television are always compiling groups of helpful hints and serving them up as TIPS. Tips are supposed to help you cope with life's little idiosyncrasies. Here are some tips that seem to surface over and over:

Springtime Tip - The Tornado

If you suspect a tornado is roaring your way, go down into the southwest corner of the basement. If the house blows away, it will probably travel off heading northeast, and the basement should stay put. If you're in a building that doesn't HAVE a basement--think up your own tip.

Summertime Tip - Heat Stroke

To avoid heat stroke in hot weather, avoid heat. Drink lots of liquids, dress thinly, remain calm and quiet and in shaded places. If you're still unbearably warm, go where it's air conditioned or sit in front of an electric fan that's turned on. (You never thought of all these innovative ideas yourself, did you.)

Electrocution by Lightning Stroke

During a thunderstorm, stay away from televisions, computers, other electric appliances, tubs, sinks, phones, windows and toilets. In other words, crawl under the bed with the dog and stay there till the storm is over.

If you're caught outdoors during a spell of lightning, lie down flat in the ditch. Ignore the stares of the people passing by.

Electrocution by Stupidity

Avoid dropping plugged-in hair dryers or television sets into the tub while taking a bath.

Stings (from Bees, Wasps, Hornets, Yellowjackets, Deer Flies and the Hordes of Other Biting, Stinging Insects)

Avoid wearing flowers, flower print material, perfume, hair spray or deodorant. Don't eat, drink or play outdoors during hot weather. Again following the good example of the family pet, snooze in the shade in a screened room till summer is over and the snow has given all the bad bugs hypothermia.

Wintertime Tip - Hypothermia

To prevent hypothermia (freezing half to death) keep warm. Turn the furnace on when you begin to see your breath as steam. Indoors, wear sweaters and long pants, socks and robe. When you're outdoors, wear outdoor clothes like coats.

If you have to walk through anything cold or wet, wear boots. Although it feels as if heat leaves you the fastest through bare feet, we're told our HEAD is where the heat likes most to desert us. So wear a hat. (I can almost hear someone saying, "DO it, stoo-pid!")

Ladies, long underwear worn beneath the dress, and a babush-ka covering the head and tied under the chin can do a really good job of keeping you warm, although some women resist good heating habits like these.

If you don't mind extra laundry, several layers of clothes keep you warmer than just one incredibly thick over-all piece. (These tips too are a revelation to the average person, who probably has often wondered how to get through a winter without hypotherming.)

Everyday Tips - Preventing Poisoning

Keep babies and other little people with no sense away from poisonous substances, to prevent accidental poisoning. (Is that the reverse of purposeful poisoning?)

Don't store your drain cleaner in a pop bottle or your insect poison in a cookie jar. Avoid leaving ashtrays filled with old butts next to the baby's crib. Get up and go SEE what Baby's up to when you hear him rummaging in the medicine cabinet.

Although it sounds like an awful lot of bother, before dosing a sick person at night, actually turn on the light, put on your glasses, and try to read the little misspelled words on the medicine's label to be sure it's the right one.

To prevent FOOD poisoning, wash your hands before you handle food. Keep animals and insects out of it. Cook it until it's done. Use clean utensils. Keep hot food hot. Keep cold food cold. After it hangs around for a few days in the refrigerator, throw it out. Repeat the whole process as needed. (Well, maybe you were raised by wolves out in the woods and haven't already figured this stuff out.)

Tips on Saving Money

Doing many small, barely significant things can save you much money in the long run. First and foremost, keep every electricity-using system turned OFF when not being used this very instant. If your spouse gets mad at you because the TV is turned off every time he returns from the bathroom, tell him what you're doing and enlist his cooperation.

Then, of course, don't complain if he follows you around in the evening turning off lights behind you.

An easy way to save WATER is to flush only after every five uses. Keep a score card on the stack of magazines next to the toilet. Also a pencil. This rule is to be disregarded when there's other than "water" involved.

Put a brick inside the toilet tank to take up room and thus use less water per flush. Get a shower head that lets only a trickle of water through, and learn to speed-bathe. If someone in the family insists on a tub bath, put several bricks in the tub to make the water deeper while using little.

To save on heating bills, turn the furnace thermostat down and keep the refrigerator door shut. As in avoiding hypothermia, wear a bunch of extra clothes. Don't open the door to let anyone in or out of the house unless absolutely necessary! Teach your dog to use the cat's litter box--dogs are as smart as cats. Aren't they?

Good Old Household Tips

Wash your clothes inside out so they don't fade on the right side. They'll only fade on the wrong side.

Before throwing out empty jelly jars, fill with hot water and shake. Use the sweetened water for making gelatine!

Always save food leftovers for later use. They can be scraped off plates, pried out of pots, plucked out of lunchboxes, frozen, and later used in many novel ways.

Add them to stew or hash, meatloaf or omelets to s-t-r-e-t-c-h those dishes. Thus you use up stale things by adding them to fresh things, both saving money and fooling your taste buds.

To make a substitute for maple syrup, cover apple, peach, pear or other fruit peels with water, add some sugar, and boil several days until it turns to syrup. Use on pancakes or grits.

Use pliers to remove the skin from a boiled tongue. (Erk. How'd that get in here?)

Keep garbage cans firmly anchored by stuffing each one inside an old car tire. This also serves to make your yard look interesting.

Make arresting flower holders: get a cracked bird bath, rusted-out barbecue, or obsolete school desk; spray paint it and sneak it into the house to put pots of flowers on.

To make a natural insecticide: chop up onions and garlic in a jar of water, let sit several days, then spray on plants. That should terrorize the bugs.

Keep a large jar somewhere in your home with eggshells and water in for watering plants. (Eggshells are supposed to do something.)

To sprout seeds in winter for planting in spring, put a small seed bed in the sunlight on the dashboard of your car. Then drive very very carefully till spring.

Mark the garden location of flower bulbs with color-coded toothpicks. Mark the location of the color-coded toothpicks with tomato stakes.

Use old nylons to tie up bean and tomato plants, to bind bundles of yard scraps for removal by trashpersons, or to inexpensively disguise the face on Halloween.

Turn the eyesore of an old swing set into a lovely backyard appendage: Hang flower baskets and a bird feeder on the overhead bar, grow flowering vines up the legs, and use the ribbons you saved from past gifts to decorate the seats.

A way has been found to get rid of unwanted ties. Make children snakes from them! Stuff the ties with old stockings, sew across each end, attach buttons for eyes, a felt forked tongue, and crocheted eyelashes. Adorable.

Make exquisite curtains by sewing together old dish towels that have perky designs and colorful colors.

Egg cartons are the darlings of tipsters; plastic or cardboard, they can be used for holding little baby socks, colored thread, lost buttons, individual jewelry chains you don't want mating with each other, your packets of frozen leftovers, or anything else small that somehow came with no container of its own.

As you save leftover food, so too save scraps of leftover material to use in stuffing toys and pillows. When your home begins to burst at the corners from stuffed toys, pillows and tie snakes, have a rummage sale!

Before discarding any old clothing, remove buttons, snaps, elastic waistbands, zippers, rickrack, etc. When you have enough of these items, make an entire recycled dress, even if everyone in the house wears mostly jeans.

Replace children's sleeper feet with pot-holders--they make durable soles. And with a bit of simple sewing, you can make potholders from the bottoms of worn blue jeans.

When the kid outgrows a pullover sweater, cut it down the front and sew it into a cardigan. When he outgrows that, make it into a vest. When that's outgrown, fashion it into a doll's dress. It'll then be virtually eternal, since the doll won't outgrow it.

Make a pillowcase from a man's worn cotton shirt. Make a kid's shirt from a worn pillowcase. Try not to forget what it is you're supposed to be making from what.

[The only problem with good old household tips is that, if you actually follow them, you soon have nothing new left to add to the old, or vice versa.

Because of thrift, lack of funds, or guilt, homemakers used to do all kinds of things like these while secretly hating them. And this is the real true reason why so many homemakers retreated from pure homemaking and went out to get a paying job. Even if the job didn't pay a lot, at least they could buy a NEW shirt, sheet or potholder, and make a FRESH pot of hash.]

Tips on Preventing Hangovers

To impede alcohol from getting into your bloodstream, eat food before drinking, preferably creamy, greasy fare to coat your stomach lining with.

Since the human body can only metabolize about one ounce of alcohol in an hour, closely watch the clock and have just one drink as each hour comes up. Do this until everyone else goes home, you fall asleep, or your liver gives out, whichever happens first.

Steer clear of bars, taverns, saloons, beer gardens and boozehalls.

At parties, entertain everyone with games, music, dancing and exciting things to talk about, serve a whole lot of delicious food, and let the pop flow like wine.

Because at long last scientists have discovered an impeccable way to prevent hangovers: don't pour alcohol into the stomach.

Allegedly, tips are concocted and assembled into a handy little bunch for your benefit. They're easy to comprehend and kinda interesting for a few minutes.

But I suspect they're intended only to fill up space in the magazines/papers and time on the airwaves. I find I always read them fast and forget them just as fast, and hardly realize I've learned utterly nothing I didn't know already.

How to Write Flawless Business Correspondence

Rule 1: **The normal way we talk has to be circumvented in business writing.**

Never write something such as "We will go to the game before the meeting." It must be "We will go to the game PRIOR TO the meeting." The same goes for "Dinner will be after the meeting." It should be "Dinner will be SUBSEQUENT TO the meeting."

Remember the photographs in magazines showing how someone looked before their diet or their plastic surgery and then afterwards? Well, they were labeled incorrectly. Rather than BEFORE and AFTER photos, they should be considered PRIOR TO and SUBSEQUENT TO photos.

Although at home we BUY and KEEP various items, in business writing we PURCHASE and RETAIN them, unless they are too expensive or COST PROHIBITIVE.

Another good prevailing word is "implementation." Aim for IMPLEMENTATION of all your company's goals. And nothing any longer has an EFFECT; even the most trivial event has an IMPACT.

"Show and tell" is only for school children. If your job involves looking up information for customers or clients, never SHOW or TELL them anything; you must REVEAL and ADVISE.

Thus, a good ready-made sentence which no one will ever be heard SAYING is "This is to advise you regarding the information our records have revealed."

Rule 2:   Use the long-established ways of writing.

This is very important. For years and years and YEARS business letter writers have been writing "ENCLOSED PLEASE FIND the information you requested." Therefore you too must write it. Heaven forbid that you should write "Here are the papers you asked for." So remember ENCLOSED PLEASE FIND. You would never speak that way, so it must be incorporated into your business letters.

Never be caught writing something such as "This letter is ABOUT your overdraft." Say instead, "This letter is REGARDING your overdraft." or "AS REGARDS your overdraft . . ." Everyone and his brother says "about" about everything, so you must never write it.

Rule 3:   To show your importance in the company, write in an imposing manner.

To do this, you must demonstrate that you know how to use ostentatious words. One fashionable ostentatious word is "utilize". Businesses utilize banks, banks utilize secretaries, secretaries utilize computers, computers utilize disks, and so on.

In real life, businesses USE banks, who use secretaries, who use computers, which use disks. But that would be too simple, ordinary and normal. Find ways to incorporate into your documents the word UTILIZATION, which is even more imposing.

A sentence such as "The machinery is old but still works well," should be rewritten "The machinery is old, however, it still works well." Although HOWEVER muddies up the sentence, it

165

sounds much more flowery than just plain BUT. Most pompous writing contains many HOWEVERs, so remember to use it often.

Pepper your letters with reflexive pronouns. That means don't write "John, Sarah and I will be coming to the meeting." You should write "John, Sarah and MYSELF will be coming to the meeting." Myself always comes to meetings. Also say, for example, "We will be giving a seminar for the staff and yourself." We like to give seminars for yourself.

Another way to show writing mastery is to lengthen words to their utmost. Thus, never say document when you can say DOCUMENTATION; the word "too" becomes ADDITIONALLY; medicine must be MEDICATION and potential becomes POTENTIALITY. Talk must be CONVERSATION, lunch must be LUNCHEON, never EXPECT when you can ANTICIPATE (2 extra syllables!), and always EXECUTE that documentation but don't fill it in.

And my favorite lengthening of all time, the word SOON rendered: IN ANY NEAR FUTURE TIME SPAN. At least, I THINK the writer meant "soon" when he wrote that.

Rule 4:   Remember that your reader may not be very bright.

For instance, he might not understand a word like "yearly" all by itself. Therefore, never say something is done yearly when you can say it is done ON A YEARLY BASIS. Also "daily" must be ON A DAILY BASIS, "monthly" ON A MONTHLY BASIS, etc.

If you are writing about hiring someone with experience, say PREVIOUS experience so that you won't get letters from people who think you might mean future experience (experience not experienced yet.)

166

Another tricky word is "proximity". Proximity means "close-ness", but to get through to someone who may be less than quick thinking, always say CLOSE PROXIMITY.

Some readers do not understand NOW. That's why important speech writers, for example, came up with AT THIS POINT IN TIME. But "at this point in time" has lost its eminence because ordinary people made fun of it. Now CURRENT must be added to everything.

Thus, if you should write "The price of our service is $100", the reader might assume that you mean your price USED TO BE $100, or that it is GOING TO BE $100. Thus, "The CURRENT price of our CURRENT service is $100." You may find it entertaining to count the number of CURRENTs in any current business correspondence you currently receive. (It's quite habit forming.)

Rule 5:   **Always brace the reader for your message before you come right out and say it.**

Never tell them anything without first writing "This letter is to advise you that . . ." That's how you first disclose you are GOING to tell them something, and THEN you actually tell them.

(This is done all the time on television, especially on the news. Consequently they don't have to put together very much news, and can spend half the news time detailing what it is they're GOING to divulge after all those commercials.)

Rule 6: **Be cautious with your reader; remember his delicate feelings.**

You must never write that someone SAID something. That person might read it and argue that they never said those exact words. You must dance around it by saying that someone INDICATED something. That sounds as though they only hinted at it, but you must remain timid of coming right out and saying that someone SAID something, even if they DID.

Although it is important to use pompous terms, you mustn't be presumptuous and bring yourself into your writing. For instance, don't say "I went to the meeting." Say "The writer went to the meeting." Even if you aren't really a writer.

If you want to seem really humble, at the very end of the letter refer to yourself as "the undersigned" and then sign your name under it. That way you avoid using those appalling words "me" and "I".

When you relate things the department or the company has done, make it sound as though no one was around at the time. For instance, "The report was written and sent out to the customers." "The documentation has been executed and the service has been started." "Your reply is anxiously awaited."

Do you see that no PERSON is mentioned who has written or has executed or is awaiting? Mentioning WHO did something might sound like boasting.

At the end of all letters you must say "If you have any questions or require further assistance on the above matter, please do not hesitate to contact me."

Don't talk like a common ordinary human being and simply say, IF YOU HAVE QUESTIONS, CALL ME.

First off, "on the above matter" must be inserted to prevent any dull-witted person from suddenly losing track of what you're talking about.

Then too, when they reach for the phone to call you, they might fearfully hesitate, nervously thinking you may yell at them for annoying you. This way they have your assurance that they NEED NOT HESITATE.

Incorporating all of the aforementioned regulations into your utilization of commercial authorship will significantly implement your vocational expectations and enhance your proficiency in procedurally meaningful characteristic habituation, if you get my drift.

How to Protect Animals' Rights

Some people who heed all the repugnant events in the daily news are becoming thoroughly fed up with the human race in general. As an outlet for their altruistic feelings then, they're turning to their fellow creatures on this planet--the animals.

This has led to many tender-hearted persons coming up with the notion that animals are more meaningful than human beings because animals don't wage war, abuse their wives, or raise food prices on welfare-check day.

If you go along with this sentiment and perhaps consider yourself an Animal Rights Activist, don't just fret about the rights of animals--get ACTIVE. Here's what you can do:

God didn't really mean it when in the Bible He told us we have dominion over animals. He only meant we're smarter than they are. He couldn't have intended that we EAT them!

So first and foremost, ban meat eating. Meat includes not only the flesh of warm-blooded animals, but also that of fish and other sea creatures, chickens and other birds, snails, slugs, and even eggs, which are infant animals such as baby chickens, baby ducks or baby caviars.

Replace traditional holiday foods such as roast turkey, baked ham, and colored Easter eggs. Delicious alternatives might be tofu and soybean dishes, and dyed boiled potatoes. Then you can release all the fowl and swine into their natural habitat out in the woods, to run loose as nature intended.

Forbid hunting. Animals should be let alone to die in their natural lingering ways--from old age, accidents, starvation, diseases, and getting eaten by other animals, but not by being shot. A bullet in the heart is not as benevolent as being torn apart by some other animal.

Blacklist everyone who uses earthworms for added protein in their cookie recipes. Powdered milk can be used for adding protein, so long as you don't take away all the cow's milk and leave none for her children.

Boycott the production, selling and wearing of animal furs, especially minks. Minks are an endangered species, like rabbits. Don't use the tail of a raccoon who died of natural causes, either. How would you like someone going around wearing YOUR hair on a hat after you're dead?

Repudiate leather, which is produced from the skin of animals. Make all shoes, gloves, jackets, saddles, seat covers, and purses from plastic.

Also prohibit silk making. You probably thought slavery was abolished years ago but, as shocking as this may be to you, silk production is still being accomplished by the slave labor of large numbers of silkworms.

It's probably all right to permit clothing to be made from cotton, so long as you don't molest the boll weevil in his natural habitat of cotton fields.

Educate humans not to vivisect. Even though cures for all kinds of human diseases and disorders have been found through live animal experimentation, that doesn't make it proper. Scientists should test germs, medicines, and mechanisms such as artificial hearts on animals that have died from natural causes. If this gives less-than-excellent results, experiment on HUMANS for human diseases. For that matter, experiment on humans for ANIMAL diseases.

Outlaw insecticides, because such chemicals murder innocent insects, which also have their rightful place in the animal kingdom. In the same vein, be careful when cleaning or repairing the home that you don't accidentally harm any spiders, cockroaches, centipedes, bedbugs, silverfish, or termites.

Also take care when plowing a field or preparing a flower bed that no worms, grasshoppers, moles, turtles, rabbits or other precious animals get frightened out of their homes by the activity.

Rather than using poisonous flea collars on your pets, hand-remove the fleas and ticks and let them escape into the grass. Then keep your pets indoors, away from fleas and ticks.

Needless to say, don't ever set a mousetrap or a rat trap, but get rid of such archaic and cruel weaponry.

If a group of hornets make a nest in your home and you can't politely get them to leave, move out until after the first few frosts have taken their toll on them, assuming you live where winter comes every year.

If you can get your Congresspersons to help, work towards the prohibition of all water filtration systems, because their procedures regularly kill millions of microscopic animals and some not so microscopic.

On the road, drive slowly to avoid killing any of God's innocent flying creatures on your grill, headlights or windshield. When walking outdoors, keep watch on where you step so you don't crush helpless little ants or worms with your big feet. Of course you probably already know enough to keep your mouth shut outdoors so that nothing alive inadvertently flies in and perishes.

Never use mothballs in your closets or luggage, because mothballs can be poisonous to our six-legged friends.

And quit the vicious habit of brushing your teeth. Tooth brushing kills and evicts little living thingies trying to set up housekeeping in your mouth.

If your female pet gets unwantedly pregnant, don't let anyone try to coerce you into getting her an abortion. It would be unfair since, being unable to voice her feelings, she would have no say in the matter. Abortions should only be performed on human females, because they are able to give informed consent to whatever invasive procedures are performed on them to either start or curtail a pregnancy.

Lastly, if you are serious in your desire to be a truly caring and compassionate animal lover, go to your doctor and have him/her disable your immune system. Unbeknownst to you, your immune system kills untold numbers of poor little creatures every day, some of which may certainly be in the animal kingdom, or nearly.

Waste Not, Want Not--Why Not

Present-day authorities assert that we who save things far past their peak of utility were brainwashed into this practice by our parents, who were all very poor and foisted their iniquitous hangups on us when we were helpless little kiddies. Don't you believe it.

Human beings are innately enamored of THINGS--always have been, probably since caveman days. Our desire to keep objects comes to us quite naturally. All our parents did was provide us with handy containers such as dolly suitcases, purses, backpacks, duffel bags and toyboxes, and suggest every now and then that we "PUT YOUR STUFF AWAY!"

Right from birth we instinctively became emotionally attached to our possessions, especially to our earliest friends, the soiled stuffed animals.

Although there came a time when we didn't want to play with them any more, sneezed and burped up on them, walked all over them, left them outside to drown in the rain, and lost them in the back of our closet under three tons of junk, we had crying fits if our parents tried to throw them away. (Gosh, Mom, do you want me to take YOUR stuff and throw it away?)

To help you in your inborn desire to save things by exploiting the wise old adages of "Waste not, want not--why not", and "A penny saved is a penny earned, soon to become a whole nickel", I present my time-tested guidelines:

Learn the art of keepsaking. Get someone to show you how to press a flower between the pages of a book, even though you'll learn later that this spoils both the flower and the book; also that you forget where the flower came from and what it's supposed to bring to mind.

But flower and four-leaf-clover pressing is an old virtuous tradition, to be handed on to the next generation with your priceless possessions.

Other keepsakes of high importance are the tassels from your graduation cap, so you remember you graduated; the cardboard parts of your wedding bouquet, so you remember you're married; and the little sticky bracelets they put on your babies so they wouldn't get mixed up in the hospital nursery, so you remember you're a parent.

To be a well-rounded accumulator, have HOBBIES. Hobbies are endeavors (such as arts, crafts, and collections) you do for fun when you're not working, and should involve a lot of THINGS. Then if you're ever bored or sick in bed, you can bring out and enjoy the hobbies you happily began in your childhood days.

As some examples:

a cigar box full of shabby seashells and sand, (say it six times fast)

a dilapidated cardboard box of paper dolls and their paper clothes with some of the tabs still intact,

a bag of dried-out magic markers and chalk butts,

a little cedar chest with gorgeous but valueless tangled jewelry,

another cigar box of stones containing diamonds (mica),

a bag of rocks containing fossils (dried mud in odd shapes),

a coffee can of marbles (some chipped, some fried),

a rubber-banded box of old coins (some real, some slugs).

Bringing your collections out and twiddling through them will give you nostalgia and pleasantly fill the time until you can go outside again.

Since you're older than you used to be and have learned the value of money and how hard it sometimes is to acquire, you'll want to save things that may not lead you down memory lane but are USEFUL, such as:

twist ties from bread bags, which are wonderful for closing off freezer bags of vegetables that you only partway use, and may have several other uses which you'll never discover if you discard any of them,

whipped topping containers which, although their lids strangely keep changing size, are so good for storing leftovers in and passing out pieces of cake or hunks of Thanksgiving turkey to your relatives to take home, whether they want them or not,

combs with a few perfectly good teeth,

pencil stubs with their erasers still nice and big,

ballpoint pen tops for future pens that lose theirs,

crumb-infiltrated bread bags to be used as free lunch bags, if anyone ever wants to carry a lunch somewhere,

rubber bands, which you never find any use for, but certainly every home should not be without.

Then branch out. If you get magazines, tear out all the important things to save, such as recipes, helpful household hints, laugh-provoking humorous articles, cartoons, instructions for building your own piano and for raising a porch herb garden if you should ever get a porch. Keep these in a drawer in the kitchen, along with your merry mountain of money-off coupons.

If you want to do it right, though, save the entire magazine. Magazines amass rapidly, so neatly box them and stack the boxes in the attic, basement, beside your dresser and under beds. You won't remember exactly what items you're saving, but you'll always know, in general, where to find them.

As time goes by, some of your little appliances will go on the fritz (i.e. malfunction or break, no one's sure which.) Place these in a pile someplace handy, like on top of one of your dead TV sets, where they can await a sudden miraculous restoration.

Your pile should include several hair dryers, a toaster, a couple of electric can openers (notorious for going on the fritz), an electric fry pan (which you don't use any more, but SOMEONE could), and numerous little pocket radios that you can only guess where they came from and who'll use them after they're fixed.

Also the bigger objects in your life will break down, such as things with wheels. These ALWAYS break, because they're used so physically. Roller skates, lawn mowers, wagons, bicycles, motorcycles.

They're all eminently fixable, so keep them until you get the time, energy and know-how to do it yourself. They are not so much to be piled up as to be leaned together over a mutual center of gravity somewhere in the garage, or behind it.

Save these things because, after they're repaired, you can SELL them and get some extra cash someday. Or, at your very laziest, you can sell them for scrap metal. Hopefully before they turn into intriguing little piles of rust.

Although you long ago quit using the garage to park vehicles in so you could store your scrap metal and other recyclables there, try to make room in the garage for keeping body parts from old dead autos, to be used in repairing the newer dead autos which are kept in the driveway.

Meanwhile, because of today's red tape, paperwork pertaining to your house, taxes, insurance, doctoring, dentisting, eyeglasses, schooling, appliances and electronic equipment is piling up at a mind-boggling rate. Not only businesses nowadays need filing cabinets. Get one. Get a COUPLE.

Stick all your new paperwork in the front of each file folder. Never throw away any paper from the BACK until you've studied it with the aid of a magnifying glass and an attorney. As you're so fond of saying every day, "You never know when you might need it."

If you have kids, or even if you don't, you should accumulate games, jigsaw puzzles, coloring books, deflated beach balls, broken-stringed racquets, scruffy checkerboards, and packs of cards. Packs and packs of cards. When the kids grow up and leave home and neglect to take their toys with them, save their things for any possible grandchildren to play with.

Clothes. It's obligatory that you save all the clothes in your closets, dressers, attic, and wherever else they're hanging or piled, even if:

they don't fit anyone in the house, because maybe next month you'll take off 30 pounds or your legs will get longer;

they are way out of style, for of course if you live long enough, the styles will come back into style;

they need mending or other fix-up job, which no one in the family has come close to doing in many a year but who knows when a fairy godmother might pop up?;

you heartily disliked them the moment you got them home and out of the bag, but maybe your daughter or son or niece or nephew will want them when they grow up.

Save old shoes, slippers and boots too. They can be fixed up and walked in once again, footed down to lower generations, or may be sorely needed if an economic misadventure takes place someday and everyone stops manufacturing footwear.

Old purses are a class unto themselves, and are so useful for keeping things in, not a single one should ever be discarded. And it's riotous good fortune to be the owner of old suitcases and steamer trunks whose sides and lids still hang together, because of the storage possibilities inherent in them.

For use in arts & crafts, keep all small useable items which somehow, luckily, missed the wastebasket. Ribbons, segments of attractive material, odd-shaped pieces of interesting gift wrap, buttons (hundreds), Easter decals with the glue long evaporated, unstrung beads of every description, brooches and earrings with the gems missing and, most abundant and meaningful, old greeting cards.

Someday you will sit contentedly with your grandchildren (if you get any) and while away many a happy hour sharing with them your knowledge of how to make wonderful items of art and craft, which they can store and save for THEIR grandchildren if there's ever a cure found for decomposition.

Rags (salvaged from used-up sheets, towels, clothing, hankies, diapers) are also important. Don't try to discriminate, just save them all, because every household should keep enough rags around to clean 10,000 cars, wipe a million oil dipsticks, and line untold pet sleeping boxes. If you keep on your toes, you'll find endless further uses for perfectly good rags.

Of course save old furniture. Someday the kids will gather up the broken legs, scrape off the spiderwebs, mouse turds and mold, and make use of this money-saving stockpile you've stored all those years.

As you may have realized, you must buy more things as you go along in order to continue to procure things to save. That's why price-drop sales were invented--incentives to get things while the getting's good.

179

So get out there and grab up those surprisingly low-priced knee-high nylons, bath mats, window-wash fluids, screw driver sets and small cans of water-packed tuna.

Don't waste precious time searching through your living area trying to find how many of these things you already have stored up against a sudden price jump, or you may miss out on the sale!

Just like in every other area of human activity, men and women are different and have their own unique reasons for wasting-not.

Women, being loving and feeling, keep things for sentimental reasons. Each item was a gift from a loved one, was unearthed with great good luck at a flea market, was acquired near the time of some memorable occurrence in her life (such as when she took off ten pounds or when she first glimpsed Niagara Falls), was her grandmother's, or her kindergartner made it for her.

She also cares deeply for things whose only function is being "pretty" or "cute". (These are words that, oddly, men have never been able to grasp the significance of.) Thus She ends up with the greater NUMBER of articles.

Men, being insecure, future-oriented and money-grubbing, keep things because they imagine they'll someday actually USE them in a worthwhile way, either saving money or making money. (You can see this is MUCH better than keeping something just for sentimental reasons.)

No object every reaches the trashcan until it's been stripped of everything useable on its entire being. This way, usually nothing much reaches the trashcan but is stored, piecemeal, in clusters in the garage, basement, and various storage sheds. Thus He ends up with the greater AREA SIZE of articles.

It will be noted that, although they each have an equal hoard of things past their peak of utility, she thinks of his stuff as junk and he calls hers crap. If the two are married to each other and care to stay that way, they may badmouth the other's things but must never touch them.

At last we come to what every wishful-thinking thingkeeper loves: COLLECTORS ITEMS. They're easy to determine--if an object looks like it might have been kicking around before 1970, it's an antique. Antiques, of course, are collectors items, and everyone knows collectors items are VALUABLE. Examples are rampant:

old yellow magazines that were once white but still have some legibility,

old books to which the covers still partly adhere,

old papers or drawings from someone's old schooldays, which surely must be historically significant,

old photo albums of old unnamed ancestors,

anything old.

There are two ways you can go with antiques. You can display them on shelves, tables, cupboard tops and window sills to awe visitors.

Or, since these sites are already taken by your newer objects, you can store your valuable collectibles in a sheltered spot in the attic, where antique collectors will be sure to see them if those collectors ever happen to be burgling in your neighborhood.

One last bit of information: there's a new occupation called "clutter-busting". The clutter-buster is a semi-professional who tries to get paid to go into homes and tell people which of their treasured possessions are clutter or litter. This is supposed to make the owner look at his things in a new way and suddenly decide he doesn't want them after all. Fat chance!

How to Treat Your Secretary
(Assuming She's Female)

• **Provide Her with Quiet, Pleasant Working Conditions**

To maintain a friendly atmosphere at your place of business, have impromptu conferences and hilarious banterfests while standing by your secretary's desk or, preferably, directly behind her chair, wherever your noise will interfere the most with her concentration and phone ear. Try to plant yourself and your fellow chatterers where she'll need to squeeze past if she has to leave her desk.

Always compose your instructions and typing assignments in hieroglyphics, writing real tiny with a blunt pencil on yellow paper. Or else use a black marker whose letters spread out and leak into one another, for ease of scribbling but difficulty or impossibility of deciphering.

Expect her not only to decipher this but also word-process and print it, using a new black ribbon so you can READ it.

• **Provide Her With an Interesting Variety of Jobs**

Typing

When she gives you the papers she typed up from your written or dictated words, be sure to change the wording and rearrange the sentences. After she's made these changes, proceed to find your own errors and omissions you should have noticed the first time but didn't. Scrawl your alterations and instructions all over the pages, again using your dull pencil or mushy marker. Expect her to make heads and tails out of it.

When the paper has been done over enough times to finally pass your inspection, hand it around to other people for THEIR opinions and alterations. At long last, when only one little comma has to be changed, circle it in ink so she'll have to redo the whole page and not just change the little error. You don't want her getting lazy.

Spend the morning chatting with your peers, pretending it's important work-related dialogue. Spend the early afternoon lunching with customers or clients.

Around 3 or 4 o'clock, begin putting together the project that all of a sudden has to get out tonight. Smile brightly and present it to your secretary 20 minutes before the time she usually runs out the door to catch her bus.

A variation of this is to write at home all evening; when she comes in the office door at 8:00 a.m. the next day, present her with 17 pages of scribbles that have to be typed up for today's 8:30 a.m. meeting. Pretend you didn't know ahead of time about this meeting that's been held every month for the last 9 years.

Telephoning

When you read the telephone messages she takes for you, don't call the persons back until you've quizzed her. "Did this man say why he was calling? Did you tell him I was only down the hall and was returning in three minutes? Did my wife sound like she was upset about something? This says 'my sister.' WHICH sister--I have three. Whenever this Major Eminent calls me, don't take a message--come and find me! You know where the men's room is."

Have your spouse and various members of your family call you several times a day, just to give your secretary practice in using her phone etiquette. Even though you spent all of last night and early this morning with your spouse, let her or him know you ENJOY hearing about every little thought that passes through their mind during the day.

Also that best friend you always eat lunch with in the cafeteria at noon--instruct them to call you once or twice every morning to explain anew when and where to meet for lunch. Secretaries get a big kick out of taking identical useless messages every day.

Even when you're right there in your office, have your secretary make phone calls for you. This creates fruitless three-way conversations, where the person on the other end of the line asks her something she doesn't know and she has to go to you for the answer, then back to them, and so on.

It's inefficient and pointless, something like having your own valet. But it makes the people on the other end of the phone presume you're IMPORTANT if you have a secretary make your calls for you.

When everyone else is at lunch and you find her trapped at the switchboard, give her a complicated long distance call to make for you. Let HER figure out how she's going to do this without putting the long distance person on hold while she answers the incoming calls, or ignoring the people trying to call in while she converses long distance.

Making Reservations

Have her make reservations for you. If it's a plane reservation, be sure to tell her the important facts: where you're going and when you want to leave. Forget to tell her when you want to return.

If it's a restaurant reservation, tell her how many people will be dining, and what time, but carefully neglect to tell her whether it's to be smoking or non-smoking.

Most important, after she's labored to collect all the data and finally made the reservations, change your mind about some facet of the plans. Blame it on your clients changing THEIR minds.

Running Errands

Just before she leaves for lunch, think of an errand that desperately needs to be run and that only she can handle. Surely she can give up her mundane lunch plans for the sake of the entire company's important business!

Keeping Your Appointment Schedule

Keep her informed of where you are at all times so she'll know what to tell all those people trying to reach you. When she's on the phone with a client is a good time to dash out the door, proclaiming over your shoulder where you're going and when you'll return. It's comical to see her try to catch your words in one ear and the phone words in the other and mess up with both.

Filing

Save every document (piece of paper) that enters your department and several copies of everything you send out. Don't let even five-word memos get away; you never know when they might be needed.

Have your secretary file this paperwork alphabetically and by date, a job that even a third grader could take care of if only they had nothing else to do and the paper didn't pile up at the rate of 7 pounds per day.

Correcting Problems

Bad things happen to postpone getting important work out the door, such as: someone spilled coffee on the courier supplies and now they're all glued together, the copier jams, the computer develops rigor mortis, the printer ribbon splits, the toner cartridge pops a leak, everyone in the building runs out of paper at the same time. These things take time for the secretary to try to set aright.

So reserve all important work until late in the day. This way everything will be hurried and error-prone and you'll have something to dredge up when review time comes and you want to hold down costs on raises. At least, that MUST be the reason--no one has yet come up with any better explanation for why things consistently get put off until the last minute.

Fetching Meeting Food

Morning meetings require breakfast bakery; afternoon meetings require sandwiches and potato chips; all meetings require gallons of coffee, hot water, tea bags, and little sweetener packets. Send your secretary for these refreshments. She'll enjoy getting a break from her work to go out and bring back a squeaking cart holding tippy pots and drag it into the conference room.

And make sure she gets a chance at the leftover food when the meeting's over. She'll appreciate your thoughtfulness.

- **Provide The Female Secretary With Higher Pay Than The Male**

Reasons

♀   A woman wears dresses and skirts with tops, plus jewelry to complement each outfit, of which she must have an unlimited variety. Even if her clothes are in high style and perfect condition, she must not be seen in the same outfit more than once a month.

♂   A man wears a dark jacket and pants, a plain light shirt and a boring tie. So long as the suit's clean and not shabby, no one cares or even can TELL whether he wears the identical one every day. Same goes for the shirt and tie.

♀   A woman wears sadist-designed shoes, with little stilts below her heels that cause gravity to squash her toes into the front which forms a long narrow point. No human's feet ever grew that shape. She makes the income of podiatrists the envy of the medical world.

And it's essential her shoes match her extensive wardrobe--red with red, grey with grey, blue with blue, brown with brown, and taupe or black or white with everything else. Twelve pairs, minimum.

♂   A man wears comfortable foot-shaped shoes with heels the height God intended people to walk on. He contentedly gets along with one black pair, one brown pair. That's two pairs, max.

♀   She wears pantyhose, which are constructed to deteriorate into ugly runs at the rate of one set of hose per week. They can't be repaired, and the hole always runs to where it shows. Therefore, she has to buy 52 pairs of pantyhose a year.

♂   He wears socks, as durable as his shoes. No one can see if he springs a hole in them anyway because his pants cover them. So he gets by on 5 pairs of socks a year (one for each workday of the week).

♀ She gets a monthly hairstyling and a weekly hairDO at a beauty emporium. To keep up the DO, she has to use hair spray, mousse, or both. Lotsa bucks.

♂ He gets a haircut at a barbershop every now and then. To keep up his hairdo he needs a comb. Pennies.

♀ Each morning she must apply skin, eye, cheek and lip makeup. (Eyeliner alone costs $7000 a pound.) At night she has to remove all that gunk, and some of it won't come off with just plain washing, so she needs a special remover and bales of cotton balls.

♂ He washes his face each day. He needs a bar of soap.

* * * * * *

So if you really want to treat your secretary, be sure to tell her repeatedly how much you appreciate her. Then take her seriously when she says, "Cancel the praise--give me a raise!"

Eating-Out Etiquette

Eating in public, such as at restaurants and dining halls or anywhere else strangers can see you, is different from eating in the privacy of your own home. In public all eyes will be on you, inspecting your every move to discern whether you commit some absurd disgusting blunder.

So that you'll never again humiliate yourself in front of large numbers of strangers as you most certainly have done in the past, here are up-to-the-minute rules on the critically important subject of eating-out etiquette:

If you're hosting someone and are being led to your seats by the Maitre d', allow your guest to walk in front of you. This way, if there are any grease spots or rug lumps on the floor, the guest will slip or stumble ahead of you and you'll be able to avoid such awkwardity.

When you get to your chair, glide symmetrically into it. Don't flop down and drag the chair up closer to the table with several little struggling jerks. People will think you're from the boondocks. If you need to get closer to the table, inch your chair forward imperceptibly until you get where you want to be.

A rule of thumb is to sit two thumb-lengths from the table. This ensures that you aren't squeezed against the tablecloth, dislodging it with your every move, nor so far from your plate that you keep bouncing dropped food from your lap to the floor.

Don't rearrange glasses, plates, silverware, flowers or ashtrays. Whoever set the table knows better than you how things should be placed. Mainly you don't want people to mistake you for the hired help.

Don't rest your arms on the table while dining. You take up too much of other people's space that way. How can they get their fork up to their mouth if your arm is in the way? When dining alone, place both arms entirely on the table so that no stranger will try to sit down beside you.

If you're someone's guest, let your host put his napkin on his lap first, before you do yours. You want HIM to be the one who appears impatient to start stuffing himself, not you.

If you find your napkin sticking up out of a glass, that's a signal for you to leave the napkin alone and wait for the waiter to come and place it on your lap. His putting the napkin on your lap is a signal for you to remember to tip him.

Don't use your napkin as a bib. Bring a bib with you from home if you need one. And keep your napkin folded approximately in half. It isn't necessary to open it up all the way and spread it down over your shins.

A really fastidious diner will keep their napkin spanking clean, so wipe off all your lipstick on a tissue before the meal. If you're a man, remind any female tablemates to clean off their lipstick before they dig in. If you should happen to need to USE your napkin, furtively dab your lips, don't rub and scrub.

If something really gluey gets stuck all over your face, ignore it until you can get to the restroom. Since most restrooms have only hot-air hand dryers and no paper towels, it's only common sense to bring a wash cloth and towel with you in your handbag or briefcase when you eat out.

You should avoid leaving big greasy lip prints on your glass for other people to have to look at, so gently blot your lips before drinking. Also after drinking, to catch chin dribbles.

When you leave the table, place your napkin to the left of the plate, or on your chair. Don't wad it up into a ball, because it will fall open no matter how hard you squeeze it shut. Don't put it on your plate either, because it will get snarled up in your scraps and cause difficulty for the busboy.

When not sitting on your chair, push it under the table. Don't leave it in the aisle for people to knock into, or you may come back and find it got bumped so far out of place you don't know where it went.

Don't blow your nose on your napkin. Don't blow your nose on ANYTHING when sitting at the table. It may sicken the other diners to hear a nose being emptied, so again go to the restroom and relieve your nose on toilet tissue. If someone in the restroom doesn't like the sound, that's THEIR problem. That's where repulsive sounds are SUPPOSED to be made.

When dining in a formal setting where there are numerous forks, knives and spoons at each place, begin using the flatware that's farthest from your plate. Take care not to pilfer some of your neighbors' in case he's the vicious type who can't tolerate a little innocent stupidity.

Never cut more than 3 bites at a time. Then if you get full and still have some of your entree left, it will be in one piece and easier to place into the doggie bag.

If you should need the waiter during the meal, don't snap your fingers, clap your hands, clang on a glass with a spoon, or wave your napkin around like a flag. Use elegant gestures, such as: nod your head, hold up your hand and point a finger to the sky (not the middle one), gently say "exCUSE me", or stand up with your handbag in your hand and pretend you're about to leave without paying. These elegant gestures should quickly bring a waiter to your side.

Always pass to the right of your position. If the person on your left asks you to pass something, send it around the table toward your right until it reaches them.

Salt and pepper should always be passed together. If someone says irritably "I only asked for the SALT!", raise your chin and look down your nose at them, indicating that you're a person who knows what is correct but they certainly aren't.

When salt cellars are on the table, use the tip of a knife, your fingers, or a salt spoon to get an amount of salt approximately the size of two shakes. You must never pick up the salt cellar and try to shake some salt out of it onto your food. Invariably you'll be inundated with sodium and have to send your food back to the kitchen, risking that they'll simply rinse it off and bring it back soggy.

Speaking of sending food back to the kitchen, this is one of the most important things to do if you want to favorably impress all those people watching you. It shows you're a person to be reckoned with, one who will not be taken advantage of, one who does NOT tolerate food that isn't perfect. So if your steak has one drop of blood too many, or the sour cream isn't sour enough, or your salad has an aphid in it, send it back!

The cream pitcher and gravy boat should be passed with their spouts facing the person you're passing them to so that, if they should overflow, the slop will land on the person pestering you for the cream or gravy, and not on you.

When you discover a bread basket in front of you, pick it up and offer it first to the person on your right. This is to impress everyone with your princely generosity and unselfishness.

When you then get a roll for yourself, never seize it, butter it, and begin to eat it. This shows everyone that you've forgotten where you are and imagine you're back home in the hills. You must follow these precise steps:

192

1) Break the roll in half,
2) Tear off one bite-size piece,
3) Butter that piece, taking great care not to butter your fingers,
4) Put down the butter knife on the bread plate,
5) Place the piece entirely into your mouth,
6) Chew it up.
7) Repeat steps 2-6 until something more interesting to eat comes along.

Do not ever lick your fingers, not even the tips, not even if there is melted Belgian chocolate on them.

When you're served a bowl of soup, lean forward slightly, spoon away from you, and sip from the side of the spoon, not the tip. If you sip from the tip you'll have to turn your arm at an awkward angle and run the risk of getting your elbow accidentally bitten by your neighbor.

Never never slurp. If eating soup makes you nervous because you find that it always runs down your chin unless you slurp, simply keep your face over the bowl, letting whatever runs down proceed back into the bowl, until you've finished. Then blot your chin, neck and chest with the napkin.

Deal with a salad the same way you deal with meat--don't simply cut it all up and then eat it, like a hog at a trough! You must cut it only one or two bites ahead of putting it into your mouth. If a big green leaf should inadvertently be picked up by your fork, don't gnaw some off, lest someone chide you for behaving like a rabbit. Quickly drop it back into the bowl and cut it twice before again trying to get it into your mouth.

Never blow on a hot drink. Instead, take 1 or 2 pieces of ice from your water glass and stir them into the drink. Blowing on things causes your breath to get on other people, and some persons are offended by that.

Never drink directly from a can or a bottle, especially a two-liter one. You might spill it down your front or get your tongue caught in it and embarrass yourself.

In Europe you get tea in a pot, fully brewed and ready to drink. In America, we're addicted to using little paper bags with string handles on to make tea in our own cup. When the tea looks dark enough to be drinkable, lift out the bag and squeeze it between a fork and a spoon, then place the ugly little thing on your saucer.

If you're using a mug, (for some reason mugs don't have saucers) place the used bag on your bread & butter plate. If there's nothing left on the table to use besides the tablecloth, smuggle the teabag into your purse. If you don't have a purse, flip the bag under the table when you think no one is looking.

Never use an ashtray as a waste receptacle for sugar wrappings, lemon wedges, cherry pits or gum. If you can't find a nearby wastebasket, slip the litter under the edge of your plate. Never use an ashtray as an ashtray, either, because smoking is considered public harassment by many breathers nowadays.

Wine is so socially correct, it has its own rules:

Red wine is to be served in a 1/3 full goblet and drunk with red meat or cherry gelatine.

White wine is served in a 1/2 full goblet, to be drunk with chicken, fish, veal in cream sauce, or mashed potatoes.

Rose' wine is served if both white and red meats are on the menu, and at baby showers for girl babies.

Yellow wine is served at meals featuring scrambled eggs, buttered squash, or lemon pie. Green wine is ONLY correct at St. Patrick's Day celebrations.

There are even rules about what glass to use:

Champagne is served in a large water glass and can be drunk throughout the entire meal.

Red wine is served in a glass with a round bowl having a short stem. To pick it up, place your thumb and first two fingers at the base of the bowl. Pinch hard so that it doesn't tip right over when you try to raise it. This kind of glass lets the wine get warm from your hand, so serve red wine at room temperature. If warm red wine makes you gag, just PRETEND to drink it.

White wine should be served chilled and is therefore served in a glass with a longer stem. Place your thumb and first two fingers at the base of the stem. This is REALLY hard to do without letting the glass tip, but your fingers should never touch the bowl--warmth affects chilled wine. It makes it warm.

Know how to eat difficult foods before you ever enter a restaurant. Oddly enough, you're allowed to eat bacon with your fingers if crisp. The bacon being crisp, that is, not the fingers. If it isn't very crisp, use a fork. If the bacon is flabby, you aren't required to eat it at all, because someone must have forgotten to cook it.

Artichokes can be eaten with ease if you follow these simple steps and enjoy eating such peculiar fare. Tear off one leaf at a time and pull it between your teeth to get the solidness. Then push aside the pile of prickly leaves and eat the heart with a knife and fork. The heart is that small piece left after the leaves have been skinned. Artichokes are good for appetizers, because working that hard for such a minimal amount of food makes many people ravenous for something that actually contains CALORIES.

Grapes should be removed in small twigs, then pulled off just one at a time. If you try to pull them off a handful at a time, you'll get stems in your mouth. Stealthily spit any seeds into your hand and sneak them onto your plate. It's best not to spit-blow them off your tongue because they might accidentally sail into someone else's food and incite a terrible scene.

A lemon wedge you want to squirt onto fish or into iced tea must first be pierced with a fork until it begins to bleed. Then squeeze it while cupping it in your hand. To use the juice that's all over your hand, briskly shake your hand over the fish or iced tea.

Escargot in shells are served with tongs, which are held in one hand, and pulled out with a fork in the other hand, for eating with another hand. Maybe one of your table neighbors can help you accomplish this.

Fried chicken must be eaten with cutlery, unless your host does otherwise. If you're the host, do otherwise.

Ice cream must be eaten a complete spoonful at a time. You've surely seen people who pick up a big gob of ice cream on their spoon, put it into their mouth, pull it back out with the lump a little smaller, put it back in, pull it back out with the goo even smaller. You get the picture, and it isn't a pretty one.

Garnishes are silly little finger foods that must be eaten elegantly. The only way to do that is to consume them in one bite without nipping your fingers. Especially a cherry tomato, because if you try to cut it, it will either squirt its seeds all over you or fly off the table.

A shrimp is eaten in one bite unless it's too large. If you're not sure how many bites are correct, look around the table and make note of how many bites others take. It also depends on the size of your mouth and whether you want to risk choking (with concomitant coughing, hacking and copious drooling) if the bite is too big.

Spaghetti is eaten by placing your fork at an angle and twirling the strands on the side of the plate. Don't use a spoon to twirl it in. That would make it too easy.

Pate is sliced off in perfect squares and lifted with your knife onto toast. This is quite a feat, since knives are not only sharp but notoriously slippery. That's why spoons and forks were invented.

Barbecued ribs or chicken must not be ordered in public when you wish to impress people. If you're a low-class type who eats out just to impress your stomach, order a big basketful of ribs or chicken. But don't expect people ever again to invite you to state or royal dinners.

Keep toothpicks out of the picture and away from the dining room. Use your fingernails to pick food out of your teeth until you've paid the bill and are on the way to your car. That's the only time it's polite to use a toothpick.

Don't dip your napkin into the flower vase to get water to wash out a stain on your clothing. When you go to the restroom to wash your face, blow your nose, floss your teeth, and allow burps to rise, you can then launder your clothes of any food spots before they terminally congeal.

Don't put liquid into your mouth if food is already occupying the space. Don't put food into your mouth if liquid is already occupying the space. Either way, when you open your mouth something is bound to fall or leak out. Swallow one mouthful at a time, thank you, before entering another one.

There are two exceptions to this rule: having peanut butter stuck to the roof of your mouth, or having chewed a mouthful of saltine crackers and no saliva has developed. Then you may add some liquid to the mouth if you do so unobtrusively.

The highest rule of public eating is: Never let anyone see food being processed in your mouth in preparation for swallowing. The best way to prevent such an offense is to chew with your mouth closed. Don't forget to open it again for the next bite. We're talking precise timing here.

Don't shovel food in. Spoon it in, fork it in, or finger it in, but don't shovel it in. If you find a shovel in your place setting, simply disregard it.

To be a cultured human being you must master another diffi-cult maneuver, like the one you learned about eating soup without slurping: you must learn to carry on friendly conversation while at the same time eating your meal before it gets cold and before every-one else is done and muttering at you to "finish already!" so they can order dessert.

Conducting mealtime conversation is a very difficult under-taking because of these rules:

Don't talk with food in your mouth. Speaking causes small wet segments to spew into the face of the person you're talking to.

Don't then talk with your HANDS when you're eating. Wav-ing food, drinks, and cutlery around causes your tablemates to become targets for even larger segments, coffee burns, icewater baths, and prong punctures.

Keep up the conversation but stay away from interesting topics such as housebreaking your dog, sewer backups, or surgery proced-ures and scar size. Childbirth traumas are all right to talk about if everyone at the table is a woman.

Don't talk about diets, because this puts a damper on the fes-tivities since everyone is at that very moment breaking their latest diet.

To avoid looking like a bumpkin, don't reach any farther than the far side of your plate. If you need something beyond that limit, let the person next to you stretch and strain to get it for you. If he refuses to reach beyond the far side of HIS plate, try coaxing the person on the other side of you for help. If that doesn't work, you can either call the waiter or do without. Drinking your coffee black won't kill you.

Don't clink your spoon when stirring a drink. This could bad-ly upset any nervous soul nearby who may have delicate sensibilities and an overly acute sense of hearing. For the same reason, don't smack your lips, even if you accidentally bite into a lemon wedge. Don't burp aloud. Cultured people release gases silently.

Don't sneeze with a mouthful of food; that's only cute when little tots do it on a home video. And always ask for permission before you pick food off someone else's plate.

Don't mash food together, stir it around and around, or make railroad tracks in it with your fork. That's only to be done when you're served something you can't stand and you want to make it look as though you've eaten some of it.

Don't dunk. Dunking can cause large chunks of food to drop into your drink and startle you later when you're finishing the drink. Dunking will also cause liquid to collect on your fingers and run down your elbow when you raise the dunked object to your mouth, and that feels really disgusting.

Be courteous and actually look at the person trying to serve you. Don't treat them like they're intruding on your conversation. They're there to make a living wage. You're there to eat and get out.

Don't comb your hair or powder your face at the table. Hair and powder have a tendency to waft. Discreetly hide behind a pocket mirror when you're applying lipstick or mascara or examining your teeth.

Pace yourself with your guest, so that you're not all done and your plate gone, while your guest is hastily trying to cut and chew before his plate gets snatched.

Don't thrust your plate away when you've had enough. Only tots in high chairs do that. And they get smacked for it.

Don't stack the dishes or clean up in any way. If you want something to do because you're bored waiting for the others to finish, look around the room and try to spot people making asinine etiquette blunders the way you used to do.

If you're hosting, arrange ahead of time to have the check given to you, unless you forgot to bring along enough cash or credit. In that case, allow the bill to lie on the table until someone else finally picks it up because they see the cleaning crew turning out the lights and stacking the chairs.

Don't whip out a calculator or a pen to check the bill's accuracy. Do it with a pencil on an out-of-the-way corner of the tablecloth.

Lastly, there's the distasteful matter of the tip. Some diners find calculating a percentage of a number a complicated chore. So to be helpful, certain restaurants automatically add a percentage onto the bill for the tip, thereby freeing the customer from having to grapple with it. But this leaves customers with no choice, effectively coercing them into tipping no matter what kind of service they got.

Regardless of how the public thinks it should be or would LIKE it to be, the immutable rules are these: tip 15% for a normal meal (the food poor, the service bad) and 20% for a spectacular meal (the food good, the service O.K.).

Tip nothing at all if everything was awful or if they gave you a table just outside the men's room. Leaving a quarter on the table for an insult tip is ill-bred, and also squanders a perfectly good quarter.

How to be a Beautiful Woman

There is a place in Gagaland called The World of Beauty. The basic teachings of The World of Beauty are these:

Women* who are beautiful do not have troubles and are wholly happy.

Makeup will make you beautiful.

Therefore, use makeup and you will be happy.

What could be more simple.

(*For our purposes, a WOMAN is any female person over the age of ten years. 11-year-olds have been known to be ostracized for not wearing makeup.)

Your only obstacle might be that ideas of what's beautiful change from time to time; so if you're a woman of discrimination, you will want to keep alert to FASHION. One way to do this is by reading the just-for-women magazines. Then you'll never be at a loss over what to spread on your face. Without the articles and advertisements on cosmetics, some of these magazines would be fashionably thin indeed.

NATURAL is a big word in The World of Beauty. It's a dirty word when referring to an un-madeup face; only careless sloppy women go natural. But "natural" is a nice word when referring to your makeup. You should allow only NATURAL makeup on your delicate face, not some chemical conglomeration.

(Disregard the fact that cyanide, hemlock, lead and arsenic are completely natural entities. I've read that manufacturers quit putting poisonous substances into cosmetics YEARS ago.)

You then, surely not wanting to be a slob, need to know the most up-to-date rules from The World of Beauty.

The fundamental concept: try to make everyone notice you, but do not attract unwanted attention to yourself. That is, you should try to look really distinctive, but must never be DIFFERENT from other women.

One way to follow this bewildering rule is to take up the latest weird beauty fad only after your best friend or favorite female singer has begun to use it, but before every copycat in town has discovered it.

There are many "looks" in The World of Beauty. Taking your cue from the beautiful magazine-&-catalog models, some of the possible looks you can aim for are the Delicate Fragile, the Know-it-All Executive, the Miffed Pout, or the Gorgeouser-Than-Thou.

The two BASIC looks are the Daytime and the Nighttime. For the Daytime look, you must spend hours of your life applying makeup with the goal of having a fresh, nearly un-made-up appearance. This has to be done religiously each morning before you let anyone see you. Being late for church, school or work is no excuse.

The Nighttime look is radically different, and should make you glitter and radiate colors like you're ready for a Halloween party.

(If possible, after your makeup is in place, stand side by side before a mirror with your male partner, if you own one, and check to see if you two look like you belong to two different species. If not, you haven't used sufficient makeup.)

Night or day, the lips must draw everyone in the room's attention to them. Mainly you want men to fantasize about your mouth. So outline your lips with lip-liner, thickly fill in the outlines with garish lipstick, then pat on a bit of finishing lip powder. To keep picture-perfect, don't eat, drink, whistle, or kiss anyone.

Every woman is born with eyebrows that are either too thick or too thin, too high or too low. Therefore, the brows must either be filled in with pencil, or partially plucked out; or penciled in AND plucked out. Or let them all grow in, and position each tiny hair straight up for the surprised picket fence look.

The eyelids are to be outlined with a special pencil or paintbrush, in black or brown for day wear, seaweed or fuchsia for night. For any time of the day, apply two or three different shades of eyeshadow over the lids to give the impression that you're healing up from a couple of recent black eyes.

The lashes should be LONG (short eyelashes are revolting), so they need several thick lengthening coatings of mascara applied to them, uppers and lowers. At the same time, a special wand has to be used to SEPARATE them. Your aim is to make yourself look as though a couple of large black spiders have taken up residence on your face.

The skin needs a base coat layer of primer, with heavy emphasis on the circles under your eyes so you'll appear to have slept the night before. Next, while carefully holding your breath, powder the whole face thickly, so that any ugly skin blotches will be thoroughly submerged. The sight of a pimple or a freckle might unhinge someone who looks at you.

And if you display a dark facial mole for a "beauty mark," be advised that this affectation was banned 30 years ago. Hide it or consult a plastic surgeon.

The cheekbones must be decorated with artificial blush until you look like you're dreadfully embarrassed, have just been slapped, or are running a fever.

Lastly, take a soft brush and buff everything except the eyes and lips. You don't want to smear the non-smear lipstick or disturb the spiders.

Of course, makeup doesn't function only from your hairline to your neckline. In the category of makeup you'll also find a virtual rainbow of coloring products for your hair, fingernails, and toenails. If you like, you can apply so much RED to your various parts, you'll stand out in the crowd like an open wound.

The World of Beauty has discovered that Nature never gives a woman the proper hair color. Probably ANYTHING would be better than what you were born with. Hence, you don't have to be turning gray to use hair colorment--change your hair hue like you change your dress. Today be a blonde, tomorrow a redhead, next week a raven-haired beauty! If the hair begins to frizzle or disintegrate, switch to hair dyes that don't use harsh chemicals. They work, sort of.

As to fingernails, the goal is to look like a lady of leisure, someone who never has to change a baby, type a letter, turn on a car radio, or use toilet tissue.

To accomplish this talon-claw look, let the nails grow as long as possible, gluing on a false nail wherever you fail to grow a long enough one of your own.

Then COLOR them, with at least two heavy coats of blinding nail polish--bare nails are as unsightly as a bare face. (Of course, this only applies to women. A MAN's bare face and fingernails are quite all right. Who says life is fair?)

Undeniably, nails have their beastly problems--thinness, dryness, weakness, brittleness; and they stubbornly won't hold an enamel job without letting little pieces of it chip off, giving them the unsightly white-measles look. But, lucky for us, there are nail enamels formulated for every problem the copywriters can dream up.

There are nail polishes that will prolong their adherence to your nails, stand guard against chipping and peeling, magically force your nails to grow long faster, and make your nails as hard as nails!

Some are fortified with various enrichments such as CALCIUM and PROTEIN that are combined right with the color you spread on. This is conjectured to be an added advantage even though your nails can only absorb calcium and protein from what you eat.

Don't forget your TOENAILS. Paint them also, being careful to use a shade that matches your lipstick. But keep them trimmed short so they don't scratch any bedmate or poke up through your shoes. Even if you're perfect from head to foot, having toenails poking up through the ends of your shoes spoils the overall effect.

Outside the realm of products, but just as important to your beauty, is the tanning treatment. The World of Beauty has long decreed that white skin is OUT, that light or pale skin is quite repugnant; it's called "pasty" to betoken how unpleasant it is. Since NO woman is born with the correct skin color, even light-complexioned black women should avail themselves of tanning treatments. Counterfeit GOLDEN TAN is what's beautiful, baby!

Doctors, using scare tactics, are trying to make us quit browning ourselves in the sun OR in a tanning casket. They say that any kind of tanning rapidly speeds up the aging process and causes a profusion of wrinkles, a plethora of age spots, and skin cancer. But you certainly don't believe everything doctors say, do you?

Every week or so, get yourself a "facial," perhaps even a THERAPEUTIC facial. Various ingredient mixtures, temperature changes and massages are applied to your face, a soothing luxurious treatment that conditions and softens, relaxes and pampers you. When it's over, your face will look exactly the same as it ever did, but you'll have less money to worry about.

This same wonderful pampering treatment can be bought for your feet and your hands too, really rejuvenating your cuticles! It rejuvenates your wallet too, taking away some of its overweight condition.

Luckily, if you desire further beauty secrets, you don't have to search for Gagaland. Just go to any cosmetics counter in the mall. They'll give you the lowdown on the latest face and nail fashions, and send you home with a bagful of beauty for only one week's salary. Beauty is more important than groceries, I think you'll agree.

If you enjoyed this book and believe others would too, please use or pass on the information on this page:

ORDER FORM

Book Name: HOW TO BE A BEAUTIFUL WOMAN
And Other Vital Wisdom For You
Whatever Your Sex

No. of Copies: _____

Price Per Copy: $15.00
                +
Tax & Shipping: $ 3.00

   TOTAL: **$18.00**

(Shipping may take 1-2 weeks)

Payment by check or money order.

Send Order and Payment to:

Seven Stars Publishing
Esther Stasek
6002 W. Pleasant Valley
Parma, OH 44129

NAME: _____

ADDRESS: _____

        _____

        _____